SHARED MISSION

SHARED MISSION

RELIGIOUS EDUCATION IN

THE CATHOLIC TRADITION

Revised Edition

LEONARDO FRANCHI

Preface by Gerhard Cardinal Müller

Catholic Education Press
Washington, D.C.

Revised edition copyright © 2024
Catholic Education Press
The Catholic University of America
Washington, D.C.

First edition © 2017 by Scepter (U.K.) Ltd.

Cataloging-in-Publication Data is available from the Library of Congress
ISBN (paperback): 978-1-9498-2240-3
ISBN (ebook): 978-1-9498-2241-0

Santa Maria, Spes Nostra, Sedes Sapientiae, Ora pro Nobis

CONTENTS

PREFACE

This volume on the relationship between catechesis and religious education is a timely reminder of the importance of authentic Catholic education. As the Church of the new evangelization, we need increasingly to deepen our engagement with the many traditions and practices revealed in Sacred Tradition. Catholic religious education should help us to do this.

Our Catholic educational heritage is a gift to humanity, not just a private tradition to be cherished by the baptized. Where would contemporary education be without the influence of the early monastic communities, the cathedral schools, and the reforming energy of Charlemagne and Alcuin of York? How fortunate we are to have Saint Ignatius of Loyola, Saint John Baptiste de La Salle, Saint John Bosco, and Maria Montessori in our pantheon of educational reformers!

In Catholic schools, religious education must be grounded in Catholic theology. Wider educational theory has much to contribute to human flourishing but Catholic schools are the site of a sincere dialogue between such ideas and the principles of Catholic theology. To be a Catholic educator is to seek harmony between faith and reason, theory and practice: such a dialogue is a sine qua non of an excellent Catholic school. As the Congregation for Catholic Education has recently reminded us, contemporary Catholic schools are called to be sites of intercultural dialogue.[1] This dialogue should be sincere, rooted in tradition, and open to fresh thinking.

---

1 Congregation for Catholic Education, Educating to Intercultural Dialogue in Catholic Schools: Living in Harmony for a Civilization of Love (2013).

Catholic education, however, must have a commitment to the formation of the baptized. The wider catechetical processes of the Church are not left at the door of the Catholic school but are reshaped and applied to the life and context of a pluralistic educational body. The religious education curriculum contributes to the faith formation of the baptized by presenting the Sacred Tradition in an accessible and systematic way. Hence, religious education provides a worthy architecture for the life of Catholic schools. Let there be no doubt: it is not possible to have an effective and successful Catholic school if it fails in its provision of religious education.

In presenting the argument for *communio* as the ideal paradigm for developing the relationship between catechesis and religious education, this book offers the contemporary Church a theologically refined set of proposals to serve the new evangelization in Catholic schools. In my address to delegates gathered at the University of Glasgow for the launch of the St. Andrew's Foundation for Catholic Teacher Education in 2013, I mentioned the importance of *communio* in the life of the Church:

Communion comes about through initial conversion to the person of Christ and necessarily leads to communion with everything with which Christ is in communion.

This is the task that lies ahead. I ask all with an interest in the Catholic educational project to consider seriously the issues raised in this important volume.

Gerhard Cardinal Müller
Prefect, Congregation for the Doctrine of the Faith, 2012–2017

AUTHOR'S PROLOGUE

This book is a contribution to scholarship in the field of religious education. My aim is simple: to offer a critical perspective on the nature of religious education in the light of contemporary developments in Catholic thinking in catechesis and wider thinking in education. It is my hope that the issues raised herein will provide ample material for fruitful dialogue and constructive debate in the world of Catholic education.

I am pleased to acknowledge my scholarly debt to giants in the field. From the calendar of saints, I drew happily, and with much fruit, on the work of the following: Saint Augustine of Hippo, Saint Thomas Aquinas, Saint Ignatius of Loyola, and Saint John Baptiste de la Salle. I am equally in the debt of those who have contributed so much to recent scholarship: Josef Jungmann, Eugene Kevane, Thomas Groome, Richard Rymarz, Graham Rossiter, Jim Conroy, Bob Davies, and Stephen McKinney. I also extend my gratitude to Professor Richard Rymarz for his endorsement. This was especially pleasing given his status as a world-class scholar in the field.

I am especially grateful to Cardinal Gerhard Müller, then-prefect of the Congregation for the Doctrine of the Faith, for agreeing to write the Preface to this book. I am honored and humbled by this generous gesture.

The second edition contains some modest but necessary additions to the first edition. In the first place, the publication of the universal *Directory for Catechesis* in 2020 necessitated some revision of references and other material in the body of the text. In addition, Pope Francis's Global Compact on Education, first launched in 2019, was sufficiently important to merit an appendix to the main body of the text. Both the *Directory for Catechesis* and the Global Compact deserve further scholarly investigation.

I offer my thanks to John Martino and the staff of Catholic Education Press for publishing the second edition of this volume. I am especially grateful to the copyeditor, Greg Black, for the thorough job he did in preparing the text for publication. Any remaining infelicities are my responsibility only.

Leonardo Franchi
February 2, 2024
Feast of the Presentation of Our Lord

INTRODUCTION

This work examines the relationship between catechesis and school-based religious education as expressed in the Catholic educational tradition.[1] It offers a rationale for contemporary religious education that is both rooted in Catholic theology and informed by solid pedagogical foundations.

The distinctive yet complementary relationship between catechesis and religious education is an important theme in contemporary Catholic educational thought. A firm and nuanced understanding of the nature of this important relationship and its historical roots is essential to an authentic understanding of both fields of study.

It should not be a surprise that the conceptual framework of religious education is complex and multilayered. In essence, it can be boiled down to the following question: To what extent can the curricular subject of religious education be the primary vehicle for the faith formation of pupils in the Catholic school? When posed in these terms, are there possible lines of tension between *one* religious education curriculum offered both to pupils from Catholic families and to those who belong to other religious and philosophical traditions? Furthermore, is there a wider cultural issue regarding the role of religion in a pluralist educational environment? Both questions inform the ideas presented in this volume.

A healthy relationship between catechesis and religious education offers rich possibilities for a renewed vision for Catholic education.

---

1 Henceforth, the term "religious education" refers to a subject in the curriculum of the Catholic school unless expressly stated otherwise.

1

An authentically Catholic curriculum in religious education needs to be both grounded in Tradition and outward-facing. All pupils are invited to engage meaningfully with the tenets of Catholic thought, and to respond appropriately.

Given this high level of expectation, and in order to present a suitable way forward for policymakers and everyone with an interest in Catholic education, I offer three arguments to underpin a refreshed vision of religious education in the contemporary Catholic school:

- The relationship between catechesis and religious education can be most fully understood in broader historical and theological contexts. We need to draw from our traditions in order to move forward;
- The theology of ecclesial communion (*communio*) offers a suitable framework within which the partnership between catechesis and religious education can be developed. This offers subtlety and balance to an issue which lies at the heart of the Catholic school's self-understanding and its relationship to the wider society;
- Religious education is a dynamic partnership between principles of catechesis and principles of Catholic education. A harmonious interplay of concepts is mutually beneficial.

Addressing these claims allows us to go on an interesting journey through selected aspects of Catholic theology and the history of education. This scholarly adventure, so to speak, will shed some light on contemporary developments in church teaching and practice in schools.

We are currently living in the era of the "new evangelization."[2] There is much to be done to reclaim the intellectual foundations of

---

2   The *Pontifical Council for the Promoting of the New Evangelization*, a dicastery of the Roman Curia, was responsible for overseeing all matters related to the new evangelization from 2010 to 2022, when, as part of a wider reform of the Roman Curia, it was replaced by the Dicastery for Evangelization. See also Pope Benedict XVI, Apostolic Letter in the Form of Motu Proprio *Ubicumque et Semper* (2010), which established the original dicastery. The term "new evangelization" has been less commonly used since the establishment of the new dicastery in 2022.

Catholic education, which have been so disturbed by the advances of secularism in its many subtle yet influential guises. Religious education curricula in Catholic schools, regrettably, have not been immune to the influence of such ideologies.

Given the important role of the Catholic school in the life of the Church, the time is ripe for a fresh study of how the religious education curriculum can make an effective and lasting contribution to evangelization. As religious education provides much of the intellectual and pastoral energy underpinning the wider life of the contemporary Catholic school, it is self-evident that the Church needs to look again at how this much-contested subject area can be developed in line with authentic Catholic tradition.[3]

The later years of the twentieth and the early years of the twenty-first centuries has been a period rich in teachings from the magisterium of the Catholic Church on the topics of catechesis and Catholic education. The publication of four major church documents on catechesis underlined its importance to the contemporary Church.[4] During the same period, the magisterium published some important, if underused, documents on Catholic education.[5] Much

---

3   The use of "contested" here is important: it refers to the fact that many voices in education refuse to accept that religious education and "faith" (broadly understood) have any place in the school curriculum. See, for example, Leonard Franchi, James Conroy, and Stephen McKinney, "Religious Education," in *The SAGE Handbook of Curriculum, Pedagogy and Assessment,* ed. Dominic Wyse, Louise Hayward, and Jessica Pandya (London: Sage, 2015), 456–69.

4   Congregation for the Clergy, *General Catechetical Directory* (1971); Pope John Paul II, Apostolic Exhortation *Catechesi Tradendae* (1979); Congregation for the Clergy, *General Directory for Catechesis* (1997); Pontifical Council for Promoting New Evangelization, *Directory for Catechesis* (2020).

5   All published by the Congregation for Catholic Education: *The Catholic School* (1977); *Lay Catholics in Schools: Witnesses to Faith* (1982); *The Religious Dimension of Education in a Catholic School* (1988); *The Catholic School on the Threshold of the Third Millennium* (1997); *Educating Together in Catholic Schools: A Shared Mission between Consecrated Persons and the Lay Faithful* (2007); *Circular Letter to Presidents of Bishops' Conferences on Religious Education in Schools* (2009); *Educating to Intercultural Dialogue in Catholic Schools: Living in Harmony for a Civilization of Love* (2013); *Instruction: The Identity of a Catholic School for a Culture of Dialogue* (2020).

of this corpus remains hidden from those charged with leading Catholic schools at a local level. It is my contention in the present volume that a desire to engage meaningfully with this body of work is a sine qua non of effective and fruitful Catholic education.

Regarding the distinction between catechesis and religious education, it is essential that we do not misconstrue what is proposed here. While "'distinction'" is a powerful term, it does not here connote stark difference but an evolving relationship in which each category is able to speak to and with the other. Nonetheless, to ignore the distinction would be to indulge in a "category mistake," the consequence of which could be the development of religious education programs that are neither academically sound nor theologically robust.[6]

To be clear, catechesis is the parent of religious education. Religious education is, hence, a *legitimate development* of the content and methods of effective catechesis.[7] As it is difficult to grasp fully the implications of the aforementioned distinction without a clear understanding of the genealogy of Catholic thinking on both topics, it is necessary to explore the shifting conceptual frameworks of religious education through two lenses: the history of catechesis and certain aspects of contemporary theological, catechetical, and educational thought. This fertile and fluid framework reminds us that we are dealing with a debate rooted in the Catholic Church's distinguished theological and educational traditions.

The present volume is neither a general history of education nor a history of Catholic education. The focus is on the evolution of specific religious and educational ideas in the Catholic tradition.

6 Brendan Hyde, "A Category Mistake: Why Contemporary Australian Religious Education May Be Doomed to Failure," *Journal of Beliefs and Values: Studies in Religion and Education* 34, no. 1 (2013): 36–45.

7 For a brief overview of the challenges arising from drawing a sharp distinction between catechesis and religious education, see Joe Fleming, "Is There Anything Religious about Religious Education Any More?" in *Inspiring Faith in School: Studies in Religious Education,* ed. Marius Felderhof, Penny Thomson, and David Torevell (Aldershot, UK: Ashgate, 2007), 111–24.

Nonetheless, wider frames of reference, notably the contribution of theological investigation to developments in catechesis and religious education, influence much of the debate.

Exploring Key Terms

It is important to explore three key terms in the subject matter of the present book: *Catholic education, catechesis,* and *religious education.* What follows is not a list of fixed definitions as such but initial ideas about the conceptual borders of the fields in question.

Catholic Education

The term "Catholic education" describes the totality of experiences, instruction, formation, and support that the Church employs in order to foster the growth in virtue and wisdom of the human person.[8] Catholic education is expressed principally through a network of primary, secondary, and tertiary institutions that are governed by an educational philosophy which flows from considered reflection on Catholic doctrine.[9] The philosophy of Catholic education is rooted in a specific anthropology: the human person is created in the image and likeness of God (*imago dei*) and yet is subject to the effects of original sin.[10] The human person is in turn "loved by God, with a mission on earth and a destiny that is immortal."[11]

---

8 See Jacques Maritain, *Education at the Crossroads* (New Haven: Yale University Press, 1961). Maritain's work offers a thoughtful philosophical basis for any study of contemporary Catholic educational thought. It is fair to say that the works of Maritain are not a staple of contemporary reading lists for prospective teachers.

9 Melanie Morey, "Education in a Catholic Framework" in *Teaching the Tradition: Academic Themes in Academic Disciplines,* ed. John Piderit and Melanie Morey (Oxford: Oxford University Press, 2012), 397–416.

10 Cf. *Catechism of the Catholic Church*, paras. 356–61; Thomas Rausch, "Catholic Anthropology," in Piderit and Morey, *Teaching the Tradition*, 31–45.

11 *The Religious Dimension of Education in a Catholic School* (1988), 76.

Catholic education is more than an institutionalized or scholastically conditioned version of catechesis. Its scope goes beyond the world of religious education.[12] Catholic education claims to promote the integral formation of the whole person "by means of a systematic and critical assimilation of culture."[13]

Integral formation, as here employed, connotes a complete education of the human person: it is an application of the relationship between faith and reason to education. In Catholic education there can be no separation between acquisition of knowledge and growth in virtue. It ought to promote an openness to discussion and critical examination of a range of religious and cultural ideas in the light of both faith and reason. This allows it to remain a valid and rigorous educational experience for those who do not belong to the Catholic, or any other, religious tradition.[14]

Catechesis

"Catechesis" is the term traditionally used to describe the ongoing faith formation of the baptized. This process aims to make explicit and fruitful the energy emanating from an initial conversion.[15]

Catechesis has been normally understood as an *echoing* (or handing down) of the traditions, beliefs, and practices of the believing community. The catechetical focus in the early Church was on the oral tradition as a means of communicating the message of the Gospel.[16] Two broader questions follow: Is there value in

12 Benedict XVI, *Letter to the Faithful of the Diocese of Rome on the Urgent Task of Educating Young People* (2008).

13 Congregation for Catholic Education, *The Catholic School*, 26.

14 For a contemporary summary of some of the nuances of Catholic educational practices, see David Clayton, *The Way of Beauty: Liturgy, Education, and Inspiration for Family, School, and College* (Kettering, OH: Angelico, 2015), 55–82.

15 *General Directory for Catechesis*, 82.

16 Cf. John Paul II, *Catechesi Tradendae*; Richard Bauckham, *Jesus and the Eyewitnesses: The Gospels as Eyewitness Testimony* (Grand Rapids, MI: Eerdmans, 2006).

retaining the emphasis on orality and to what extent can catechesis as a term be used as an overarching expression for faith development?[17]

Catechesis in practice can be divided into two broad pathways: first, the postevangelization faith formation process of those preparing to enter into full communion with the Church, and second, the ongoing faith formation of the baptized members of the Church. While the former would normally operate within the framework of the Rite of Christian Initiation of Adults (RCIA), the latter can assume many different forms: homilies during church services or specific classes on a particular theme; for example, marriage. It also offers possibilities for more structured courses, possibly certificated, within the wider community of the Church. Whatever the context, pivotal to catechesis are the following: a) the assumption that faith in and intimacy with Christ is present; b) faith is developed and deepened in an atmosphere of ecclesial harmony, and c) the connection between faith formation and the liturgy is made explicit because all catechesis has full participation, properly understood, in the liturgy as its objective.[18] This liturgical aspect is particularly prominent in the RCIA process, which culminates in the reception of the candidate into full communion with the Catholic Church at the Easter Vigil Mass.

The catechetical movement of the early twentieth century sought to reenergize catechesis in the light of scholarship in both theology and education. In the years following the Second Vatican Council (1962–1965), catechesis was gradually reconfigured to refer more

---

17 Cf. Thomas Groome, *Christian Religious Education: Sharing Our Story and Vision* (San Francisco: Harper and Row, 1980); "Total Catechesis/Religious Education: A Vision for Now and Always" in *Horizons and Hopes: The Future of Religious Education,* ed. Thomas Groome and Harold Horell (New Jersey: Paulist Press, 2003); Patrick Devitt, *That You May Believe: A Brief History of Religious Education* (Dublin: Dominican Publications, 1992); Liam Kelly, *Catechesis Revisited: Handing on the Faith Today* (London: Darton Longman, 2000).

18 Second Vatican Council, Constitution on the Sacred Liturgy *Sacrosanctum Concilium* (1964), 11.

to the lifelong faith journey of the Christian person, as opposed to the approach taken in a religious education class in the Catholic school. This broader vision of the scope and purpose of catechesis prompted further discussion on whether the Catholic school was a suitable locus for a model of religious education underpinned by a predominantly catechetical framework.

Religious Education

The definition of religious education in the magisterial corpus tends to be opaque. It remains a contested term both within and beyond the Christian traditions. In broad terms, conceptual frameworks of religious education are stretched along a continuum of meaning: at one end, it is closely related to, or coterminous with, all forms of faith nurture—in other words, catechesis—and at the other end, religious education is a nonconfessional study of religious ways of understanding the world that addresses the intersection of religion and education. A fuller analysis of this debate is found in part 2.

A further distinction within the Catholic tradition is reflected in the present book's use of the terms *catechetical paradigm* and *educational paradigm* as descriptors of two conceptual frameworks of religious education. The former refers to models of religious education that draw heavily on catechetical principles; the latter refers to models of religious education that are strongly influenced by educational principles. This distinction, however, like so much in Catholic thought, lends itself to many subtle layers of nuance.

We must bear in mind, however, that we are exploring the contours of a curricular subject in a *Catholic* school. As such, it is helpful to show at this stage how the "continuum of meaning" noted above has been articulated in statements on the purpose of religious education issued by different educational agencies of the Church.

One brief example illustrates the degree of conceptual confusion that has had a significant, and not always helpful, impact on the shape of the subject. In 1986, the Catholic Bishops' Conference of England and Wales issued guidelines for religious education that reflected a model of religious education understood broadly as a study of religions and religious ways of thinking. According to this document, "Religious education is *not primarily* concerned with maturing and developing Christian faith. Its aim is to help people to be aware of and appreciate the religious dimension of life and the way this has been expressed in religious traditions."[19]

By way of contrast, the syllabus for Scottish Catholic Schools, *This Is Our Faith* (published in 2011), pushed the meaning of religious education very close to established definitions of the related term "catechesis." *This Is Our Faith* defines religious education in Catholic schools as a process that offers opportunities for both evangelization and catechesis, the latter defined in the glossary as "the religious formation of Christians."[20]

It needs to be borne in mind that these statements come from documents that are separated by a period of twenty-five years. During this time, the Church's position on the primary purpose of religious education underwent substantial modification, as we will see. Nonetheless, the divergence in thought is striking. This juxtaposition serves as a thematic signpost to the issues at the heart of the present book.

Overview of the Book

Part 1 revolves around four historical contexts selected specifically to illuminate contemporary developments in the field. While these historical periods have porous boundaries, they offer a working structure in support of the core claims of the book. The development of Catholic teaching on catechesis and religious education is an example of the interaction of change and continuity:

---

19 Jim Gallagher, *Living and Sharing Our Faith: A National Project of Catechesis and Religious Education* (London: Collins Liturgical Publications, 1986), 12.

20 Scottish Catholic Education Service, *This is Our Faith* (Glasgow: The Bishops' Conference of Scotland, 2011), 300.

each historical period, in response to evolving social, cultural, and political milieux, reshapes the tradition it has inherited. While this book does not claim to offer a global evaluation of the educational, theological, and political arguments of the selected periods, the aftershocks of these debates remain pertinent to the configuration of catechesis and religious education today.

Part 2 explores the complex genealogy of the relationship between catechesis and religious education. Key thematic frames of reference within which the relevant magisterial documents and associated academic literature are set out and explored chronologically, thus allowing for some cross-referencing across the themes—unsurprisingly the range of the issues for debate resists a neat packaging within specific time frames but does provide a helpful working structure. The four chapters of part 2 will demonstrate that the initial thematic interplay between the academic literature (secondary sources) and the magisterial documents (primary sources) led over time to the clear articulation of the distinction between catechesis and religious education in the magisterial documents.

Part 3 proposes that a "spirituality of communion" should underpin the Church's work in catechesis, education, and religious education. To do this requires mature reflection on aspects of the theology of *communio* and consideration of its implications for the Church's many formational initiatives. The term "shared mission" is introduced as a way to find a harmonious relationship between catechesis and religious education. Shared mission seems to be a satisfactory articulation of the necessary dialogic relationship between both fields and offers a suitable space for both distinction and reciprocity.

PART I

MODELS OF RELIGIOUS FORMATION:
FOUR HISTORICAL CONTEXTS

How appropriate is it to view the life of the Church at certain periods of history as normative for future generations? If we were to fall into the trap of revering the past as somehow purer and more pristine than the present, Christian belief and practice would remain rooted in what was believed and practiced at particular points in time and hence restrict theology and any form of Christian studies to the domain of historical forensics.[1] Of course, this does not lessen the value of historical study—far from it; it simply locates theology and Christian studies in a wider and more fluid framework.

Any historical study of catechetical and educational developments must take into account the relevant social and cultural contexts in which they emerged. For example, mass education, as commonly understood today, would be a concept unknown to those who lived before the nineteenth century. The limited involvement of "the child" in education and the nature of children's place in society in the past militate against drawing exact parallels between

---

1 Hubert Jedin, "General Introduction to Church History" in *History of the Church: From the Apostolic Community to Constantine*, ed. Hubert Jedin and John P. Dolan (London: Burns and Oates, 1980), 1:1–56.

particular points in history and contemporary attitudes to education and schooling.[2]

Evidence from the selected historical periods suggests strongly the predominance of the *catechetical paradigm* (see Introduction) firmly rooted in the theological and cultural resources of Catholicism. Alongside this, an *educational paradigm* gradually evolved in response to the Church's dialogue with wider thinking. To demonstrate the fluid nature of this relationship, four selected historical contexts offer important indicators of the parameters of religious formation in the Church. This offers glimpses of an evolving relationship that has culminated in the contemporary distinction between catechesis and religious education. The four selected contexts are

- Catechesis in the Apostolic and Patristic Ages (chapter 1);
- Catechesis in the Middle Ages (chapter 2);
- The Catholic Reform and Catechesis (chapter 3); and
- The Catechetical Renewal of the Early Twentieth Century (chapter 4).

---

2 For more on the place of the child in society, see the following studies: Marcia Bunge, ed., *The Child in Christian Thought* (Cambridge: Eerdmans, 2001); Odd M. Bakke, *When Children Became People: The Birth of Childhood in Early Christianity*, trans. Brian McNeil (Minneapolis: Fortress, 2005); Cornelia Horn and John Martens, *"Let the Little Children Come to Me": Childhood and Children in Early Christianity* (Washington, DC: The Catholic University of America Press, 2009).

CHAPTER 1

CATECHESIS IN THE
APOSTOLIC AND PATRISTIC AGES

Catechesis in the Apostolic and Patristic Ages, the first historical context, covers the period from apostolic times until the time of Augustine of Hippo (AD 354–430). As Augustine's writings on catechesis and educational matters form the first cohesive "philosophy" of Christian education, it is reasonable to posit his life and work as a key pivot in the development of broader Christian educational ideas.[1] Furthermore, if it is accepted that Christian doctrine and practice develop over the ages, the study of the life of the early Church offers valuable insights into the emerging Christian community's self-understanding and praxis.[2]

Owing to the paucity of relevant primary texts on the question of children's religious formation in the early Church, an element of selection is inevitable. The selected texts have to be read in the context

---

1 Cf. Eugene Kevane, *Augustine the Educator: A Study in the Fundamentals of Christian Formation* (Westminster, MD: The Newman Press, 1964); Ryan Topping, *Happiness and Wisdom: Augustine's Early Theology of Education* (Washington, DC: The Catholic University of America Press, 2012).

2 Cf. John H. Newman, *An Essay on the Development of Christian Doctrine* (Notre Dame, IN: University of Notre Dame Press, 1878/2003), chaps. 2 and 3; Gillian R. Evans, *The First Christian Theologians* (Oxford: Blackwell, 2005), 1–11.

of the wider patristic corpus, in which the writings of the Church Fathers are examples of a perceived theological freshness and energy. In this light, the catechetical paradigm of early Christian education as here presented suggests three distinct and interrelated themes.

Theme 1:
The Moral and Pastoral Formation of the Child
in Early Christianity

For the first Christians, the key educational question was one of evangelization: how to pass on their faith in the risen Jesus to those around them in response to the "great commission" of Matthew 28:19–20.[3] Indeed, all Christian thinking on education is rooted in and developed from this call to evangelize.[4]

The extant Christian writings from the first five centuries refer in broad terms to the question of children's human and religious formation.[5] They do not offer precise and practical details pertaining to this process beyond the restating of the direct responsibility of parents to rear their children in good living.[6] The lack of evidence as such is not insignificant; it shows that in early Christianity, catechesis was part of the home-centered nurturing of the child and the clear responsibility of the blood family, assisted by the wider community of believers. The contemporary understanding of Christian education as

3   "Go therefore and make disciples of all nations, baptizing them in the name of the Father and of the Son and of the Holy Spirit, teaching them to observe all that I have commanded you: and lo, I am with you always, to the close of the age." New Testament, Revised Standard Version.

4   *Circular Letter to Presidents of Bishops' Conferences on Religious Education in Schools*, 17.

5   An overview of this period is found in John P. Marmion, *Catholic Traditions in Education* (Macclesfield: St. Edward's Press, 1986).

6   Saint John Chrysostom (AD 347–407) is an invaluable primary source for early Christianity's approach to the rearing of children. See John Chrysostom, "Address on Vainglory and the Right Way for Parents to Bring Up Their Children," in Max Laistner, *Christianity and Pagan Culture in the Later Roman Empire* (New York: Cornell University Press, 1967), 85–140.

a process involving a range of dedicated establishments would have been unrecognizable to the early Church.

There is a congruence between the Jewish notion of children's religious formation and the approach adopted in the early Church. What they have in common is a set of processes centered on the home and the synagogue/Christian community with no division between the notion of education and religious learning.[7] The Jewish school system, as organized in the first century, was a way of maintaining religious and cultural identity in the face of the perceived attractions of Greek philosophy.[8] It is reasonable to suggest that the children of the first Jewish converts to Christianity continued to attend these schools and received supplementary instruction on the Christian Gospel at other times. This would align with the broader evidence that the early Christians of Jerusalem continued to adhere to their inherited forms of piety by attending temple worship before coming to "break bread" in their homes.[9]

The Gospel evidence on the place of children in the early Church community is scant but clear. Any discussion of the representation of children in the New Testament needs, of course, to be aware of both figurative and literal uses of the term "children" in the texts. Nonetheless, children are included in the groups of people who heard Jesus preach;[10] they are held up as models of humility[11] and were included, it seems, in the first missionary journeys.[12] Similarly, in the writings of Saint Paul there is evidence of the importance placed on the family's responsibility for the faith-formation of the young.[13] While the term "children" is often used in the Gospels in

---

7 Cf. Deut. 4:9; Judith M. Grundy Volf, "The Least and the Greatest: Children in the New Testament," in Bunge, *The Child in Christian Thought*, 29–60.

8 William Strange, *Children in the Early Church* (Milton Keynes: Paternoster, 2006).

9 Acts 2:46.

10 Cf. John 6:9 and Matt. 14:21.

11 Matt. 18:1–3.

12 Acts 21:1–6.

13 Cf. Col. 3:20–21; Eph. 6:1–4.

a figurative sense,[14] there was little recognition of the need to offer specific processes for children's catechesis. This is not necessarily evidence of neglect of children's religious formations; on the contrary, children in the Gospel are normally depicted as models of fidelity and receptiveness to the message of Jesus.[15]

By the late first century, the inherited (from Judaism) faith-nurture approach to education had, unsurprisingly, developed a distinct Christian flavor.[16] This approach was pastoral in nature and characterized by eager impulses to foster faith in the context of the liturgical life of the believing community. It was a Christian interpretation of the Greek concept of *paideia*.[17] This is an early and important example of the catechetical paradigm of religious education in action, so to speak.

By the late fourth century, it is possible to speak of an emerging Christian pastoral theology for children.[18] A key figure in this development, Saint John Chrysostom (347–407), argued that the raising of the child in virtue was the true end of parenthood and education.[19] As Jewish education required study of the Torah, so Chrysostom placed the study of the Christian scriptures at the heart of the educational process.

---

14 Mark 9:36–37.

15 Cf. Matt. 18:1–5; 19:14–15.

16 Cf. I Clement, chap. 1, Polycarp's Letter to the Philippians, and the Didache, in *Early Christian Writings*, ed. Andrew Louth and Max Staniforth (London: Penguin, 1987).

17 For more on catechesis in this period, see Werner Jaegger, *Early Christianity and Greek Paideia* (Cambridge, MA: Belknap Press of Harvard University Press, 1961/1977); Reinhard Feldmeier, "Before the Teachers of Israel and the Sages of Greece: Luke-Acts as a Precursor of the Conjunction of Biblical Faith and Hellenistic Education," in *Religious Education in Pre-Modern Europe*, ed. Ilinca Tanaseanu-Döbler and Marvi Döbler (Boston: Brill, 2012), 77–95.

18 Vigen Guroian, "The Ecclesial Family" in Bunge, *The Child in Christian Thought*, 61–77.

19 John Chrysostom, "Address on Vainglory and the Right Way for Parents to Bring Up Their Children," 19ff.

What makes Chrysostom's intervention crucial is that he encouraged the father of the family to use *story* as a medium to inculcate virtue in the child and, significantly, suggested the adaptation of Gospel passages to the age and intellectual capability of the listener.[20] The focus here on educational method is a modest sign of a growing Christian engagement with the human person's developmental needs in the matter of religious formation. It is a notable episode in the Christian community's attempts to develop its range of suitable educational methods. John Chrysostom's contribution is an indication of an emerging educational paradigm which moves within and is supportive of the predominant catechetical paradigm.

Such considered focus on the methods required to promote the moral and pastoral formation of young Christians was set alongside their sacramental needs. This leads to the second theme of the development of the catechetical paradigm.

Theme 2:
The Child and the Sacramental Life
of the Christian Community

There is little to suggest that the first Christians employed catechetical processes or strategies tailored specifically to the needs of children. Indeed, the lack of concrete historical evidence on the method and content of children's catechesis implies that the Church continued to view the formation of children primarily as a matter for the family, assisted by the wider church community. The liturgy

---

20 Is it possible that Chrysostom was aware of and sought to apply Saint Basil the Great's (330–379) four principles of reading Christian poetry? These principles are the hermeneutical principle, the principle of selective reading, the principle of moral development, and the principle of precaution. See Andreas Schwab, "From a Way of Reading to a Way of Life: Basil of Caesarea and Gregory of Nazianus about Poetry in Christian Education" Tanaseanu-Döbler and Döbler, *Religious Education in Pre-Modern Europe*, 147–62.

was a living curriculum through which Christian doctrine would have been taught: the Church as a worshipping community was also the Church as a catechetical community. Such liturgically focused methods, for example, allowed children to play a full part as *lectors* (readers) and singers in choir.[21] The debates over the desirability of infant baptism, alongside the rise of the catechumenate offer further examples of the Christian community's broadening of the processes of Christian formation and reflect a modest strengthening of the catechetical paradigm.

Regarding the practice of infant baptism, it is hard to ascertain the exact date of its origin. The New Testament tells us clearly that many households were baptized, thus suggesting strongly that children were included.[22] Later accounts of the development of the catechumenate and the Easter Vigil ceremonies in the late second/early third centuries state that children were baptized during the Easter Vigil along with their parents or another member of the extended family who would answer the priest's questions on the child's behalf.[23]

As the Church expanded throughout the Mediterranean basin and beyond in the first two centuries, its approach to the religious formation of the community adapted to meet these new and challenging circumstances. The *catechumenate* was the Church's response to the challenges arising from increased numbers of adults who wanted to become Christian.[24] As the demand for the baptism

---

21 Cf. Bakke, *When Children Became People*, 225; Horn and Martens, *"Let the Little Children Come to Me,"* 296–97.

22 Cf. Acts 2:38; 16:15; 16:33; 18:8.

23 For a fascinating overview of this period, see Karl Baus, "The Great Church of Early Christian Times (c. AD 180–324)," in Jedin and Dolan, *History of the Church*, 1:215–432. See also Saint Cyprian of Carthage, *To Fidus, On the Baptism of Infants* (Epistle 58:6), http://www.newadvent.org/fathers/050658.htm

24 Broadly speaking, the catechumenate was a three-year process of examination and instruction; it could be understood as a coming together of various catechetical/educational and ritual processes culminating in the sacrament of baptism at the Easter Vigil ceremonies.

of infants belonging to these families increased, adult baptism became the exception, not the norm.

Saint Cyril of Jerusalem's (314–396) catechetical lectures in the fourth century reveal the catechumenate to be a rigorous and intellectually demanding preparation for baptism.[25] While children and adults were baptized at these ceremonies, it is unclear from the available sources just how the catechumenate was adapted, if at all, to the varying needs of the children. As already noted, the paucity of available evidence suggests that the ongoing family, community, and liturgical life of the Church was the sum total of the catechetical processes for children.

In parallel with the growth of the Church, there emerged initial signs of a major development in attitudes toward other ways of thinking. The Church's encounter with Greek philosophy become foundational to its developing identity and had significant implications for its catechetical and educational actions.

Theme 3:
The Emerging Philosophy of Christian Education

The encounter with Greek philosophy was the seed of Christianity's renowned partnership between faith and reason. The early Christian apologists were willing to engage in dialogue with the wider culture on theological and cultural issues.[26] Their educational method consisted of a clearly structured apologetical presentation of doctrine to their various interlocutors.[27] It is, however, the encounter

---

25 Cyril's catechetical lectures are available in Edward Yarnold, ed., *Cyril of Jerusalem* (London: Routledge, 2000).

26 Saint Irenaeus of Lyon (130–202) and Saint Justin the Martyr (100–165) are the most famous of this group. Justin the Martyr's important contribution to the emerging tradition of Christian education can be appreciated in his dialogues, available here: http://www.newadvent.org/cathen/08580c.htm. For a richly contextualized overview of this period, see Henry Chadwick, *Early Christian Thought and the Classical Traditions* (Oxford: Oxford University Press, 1984).

27 Avery Dulles, *A History of Apologetics* (San Francisco: Ignatius Press, 1999).

of the doctrine of the risen Jesus with the intellectual apparatus of Greek thought that marks a key stage in the development of the educational paradigm of religious education as we understand it today. This is when a distinct philosophy of Christian education begins to emerge.

While a contemporary understanding of philosophy rests primarily on its identity as an academic discipline, the ancient Greeks saw it first and foremost as a way of living, with knowledge understood as a path to virtue.[28] In this respect, the Greek approach seemed to overlap with the Christian claim to truth. Indeed the New Testament actually records the initial encounters between followers of Christianity and the adherents of Greek philosophy.[29]

Within this shifting intellectual climate, the early catechetical schools—although more of a process than a physical building—became the focus of a profound cultural dialogue between Christian thinking and traditional Greek philosophy. These initially private undertakings offered an integration of religious values, philosophy, and high moral standards.[30] There is, crucially, no sense of dissonance between what the present study has identified as the educational and catechetical paradigms of religious education. It is hard, however, to identify specific indicators of the modus operandi of these institutions and of their locus, if any, in the education of children.

The most famous of these schools was the School of Alexandria. This institution allowed many members of the ruling classes in this important metropolis to attain a high degree of cultural awareness. It is not surprising that it played a pivotal role in the development of the conceptual framework of early Christian education. One of the leaders of this school, Saint Clement of Alexandria (150–215), argued that because God is the origin of all good things, the good fruits of Greek philosophy must originate in God, concluding that

---

28 Pierre Hadot, *Philosophy as a Way of Life*, trans. Michael Chase (Oxford: Blackwell, 2008). See also Topping, *Happiness and Wisdom*, 2012.

29 cf. Acts 17:16–34.

30 Baus, "The Great Church of Early Christian Times," 1:229–33.

the study of Greek philosophy was a "preparatory training to those who attain to faith through demonstration."[31]

The dialogue between Christianity and Greek philosophy had implications for Christian thinking on catechesis. The work of Augustine offers a definitive early example of the fruit of the marriage between Christianity and Greek philosophy as applied to catechesis, with glimpses therein of an emerging philosophy of Christian education.[32] His works in this field have strong claims to be among the first attempts to map out a meaningful rationale for Christian education.[33] This focus on the pedagogy of catechesis reflected the growing importance of an educational paradigm, which was gradually influencing the then established catechetical paradigm.[34]

One of Augustine's distinctive contributions to the catechetical/educational contours of the period lies principally in his work on the role of the Christian teacher. For Augustine, the teacher's role is to lead the student to the truth, understood as knowledge of

31 Clement of Alexandria, "Philosophy as the Handmaid of Theology," in *Ante-Nicene Library Translations of the Writings of the Fathers Down to AD 325*, vol. 4, *The Writings of Clement of Alexandria*, vol. 1, ed. Alexander Roberts and James Donaldson (Edinburgh: T and T Clark, 1867), 366. https://archive.org/details/writingsofclemen01clem/page/n9/mode/2up

32 Cf. Augustine, *De Magistro—On the Teacher* in *Against the Academicians* and *The Teacher*, ed. Peter King (Indianapolis: Hackett, 1959); Augustine, *De Catechezandi Rudibus—On the Catechizing of the Uninstructed* (Whitefish, MT: Kessinger Publishing Rare Reprints); Augustine, *De Doctrina Christiana—On Christian Doctrine*, trans. Durant W. Robertson (Indianapolis: Bobbs-Merrill, 1959).

33 Cf. Kevane, *Augustine the Educator*, 124; Carol Harrison, "De Doctrina Christiana," *New Blackfriars* 87, no. 1008 (2006): 121–31; Leonardo Franchi, "St Augustine, Catechesis and Religious Education," *Religious Education* 106, no. 3 (2011): 299–311; Leonardo Franchi, "Words Are Not Enough: The Teacher as Icon of the Truth in St. Augustine," in *How the Teacher is Presented in Literature, History, Religion and the Arts: Cross-Cultural Analyses of a Stereotype*, ed. Raymond McCluskey and Stephen McKinney (Lewiston, ME: Mellen Press, 2013), 191–200.

34 See Owen Chadwick, *Augustine* (Oxford: Oxford University Press, 1996) and Mary T. Clark, *Augustine* (London: Continuum, 2005) for accessible introductions to the life and thought of Augustine of Hippo.

Jesus.[35] Augustine, drawing on Clement's *Paedagogus*, saw Jesus as the
Teacher who teaches through the human teacher; it is the role of the
(Christian) teacher to point toward this truth.[36]

While John Chrysostom had recommended the use of story as a
teaching medium with due adaptation for children, Augustine promoted
the use of the *narratio* in catechesis.[37] The *narratio*, the systematic
mapping of the Christian story of salvation from Genesis to Christ, was
a key teaching method in early Christianity. It embraced all catechumens
within a Christocentric view of history in which everything would be
fulfilled in the world to come. The resultant teaching strategy, as set out
by Augustine, is a major, if understated, development in the philosophy
of Christian education. It is an educational strategy designed to use
the study of the "wonderful facts" contained in Scripture as a way to
enhance the catechetical processes in place.[38]

Augustine presented Christian education as a process by which
the sinner moves away from vice toward knowledge of Jesus and
the practice of virtue. Both adults and children were, he claimed, in
need of the grace given freely at baptism to lead them away from sin
and toward growth in virtue. While there is little in Augustine's wider
corpus about adapting catechetical methodology to children, he
advocated the adaptation of this methodology to different groups of
hearers.[39] The acceptance of the principle of differentiation offered

---

35 Augustine, *On The Teacher*, 11:38.

36 Jason P. Drucker, "Teaching as Pointing in 'The Teacher,'" *Augustinian Studies*
28, no. 2 (1997): 101–32.

37 For a critical exploration of Augustine's perspectives on childhood, see Martha
E. Stortz, "When Was Your Servant Innocent? Augustine on Childhood" in
Bunge, *The Child in Christian Thought*, 78–102.

38 Cf. Augustine, *On the Catechizing of the Uninstructed*, chap. 3; *On Christian Doctrine*
IV, V. In contemporary language, such an approach offers sacred history as
the curricular framework for the study of the scriptures in the light of the
divine pedagogy. See Petroc Willey, Pierre de Cointet, and Barbara Morgan,
The Catechism of the Catholic Church and the Craft of Catechesis (San Francisco:
Ignatius Press, 2008).

39 Augustine, *On the Catechizing of the Uninstructed*, chaps. 8, 15.

the possibility of similar adaptation for children, although this is not stated explicitly. The overall lack of concrete evidence of catechetical strategies for children once again suggests the continuation of the family- and community-centered model of catechesis. There is the possibility of children being included in the wider catechetical processes involving the *narratio*, but this does not exclude the possibility of children attending some form of "school."

The three themes outlined above reveal, unsurprisingly, a Church determined to develop the faith of its adherents. The predominant catechetical paradigm is centered on integration into its sacramental and community life. There appears to have been little explicit recognition of the needs of children in this enterprise. The dialogue between Christianity and Greek philosophy did, however, make the Church more aware of the need to make the catechetical paradigm more robust. The conceptual distinction of the twentieth century between the catechetical and educational paradigms of religious education is, at this stage, a mere shadow across the landscape.

CHAPTER 2

CATECHESIS IN THE MIDDLE AGES

Catechesis in the Middle Ages, the second historical context, covers a time when major and long-lasting developments in Christian educational thought took place. This section recognizes the influence of monastic ideals on education and explores the influence of wider thinking on educational and catechetical thought up to the age of Reformation (c. sixteenth century). The period known, perhaps unhelpfully, as the "Middle Ages" provides a set of signposts to the key themes of the present book. The changing shape of catechesis at the time marks a gradual rise of broader Christian educational structure and is evidence of the Church's continuing dialogue with other ways of thinking. It is in this period that the Christian message begins to make a significant impact on the cultural landscape of western Europe.

Liturgical and Christian Community Life as Catechesis

Two issues provide a broad cultural context for this section. First, it is hard to separate catechetical practice for children from wider societal attitudes toward children.[1] Nevertheless, as the Church continued to expand, there remains little evidence of catechetical developments

---

1 See Bakke, *When Children Became People*. Bakke's argument is that children in medieval times were recognized as more than simply "adults in the making."

specifically for children. Second, by the seventh century, the collapse of the western Roman Empire and the demise of its intellectual patrimony had left very low levels of literacy throughout the lands of its former empire. This state of affairs required the Church to organize its catechetical methods in ways that would be effective for the minimally educated majority of its members.

Crucially, the Church was where people increasingly found the key to the meaning and purpose of their lives.[2] Dedicated catechetical processes were part of the ways in which people absorbed the Catholic faith.[3] Although Paul had said in Acts 17:24 that God does not dwell in sanctuaries made by human hands, places of Christian public worship grew from the initial Christian homes and Roman *tituli* into a network of churches.[4] Some medieval church buildings were designed to resemble the heavenly Jerusalem, with their physical structure and design wholly in keeping with the high eschatological ideals represented by liturgical worship.[5] The Romanesque and Gothic churches and cathedrals became instruments of catechesis— the so-called "stone bibles"—and examples of architectural beauty as pathways to the divine.[6] The liturgical rites performed within and

---

2 For a fascinating study of how the Church was an intrinsic part of the life of the people of England before the English Reformation, see Eamon Duffy, *The Stripping of the Altars: Traditional Religion in England c. 1400–c. 1580* (New Haven: Yale University Press, 1992).

3 It is helpful here to distinguish between how the faith is *taught* and how the faith is *learned*. The former connotes explicit methods designed to teach; the latter includes the more formal aspects of teaching but occurring alongside the recognition of wider social and cultural influences on the formation of faith. For more on this, see Kevin E. Lawson, "Learning the Faith in England in the Later Middle Ages: Contributions of the Franciscan Friars," *Religious Education* 107, no. 2 (2012): 139–57.

4 Karl Baus, "The Beginnings," in Jedin and Dolan, *History of the Church*, 1:146–52.

5 For a helpful overview of the relationship between architecture and religious faith, see R. Kevin Seasoltz, *A Sense of the Sacred* (New York: Continuum, 2005).

6 Benedict XVI, "The Cathedral from the Romanesque to the Gothic Architecture: The Theological Background," General Audience, November 18, 2009.

beyond these walls underpinned both the religious formation and the daily life of the Christian community, although there is a need for caution in drawing too sharp a distinction between life within and without the walls of the churches at this time. In late medieval Europe, the religious atmosphere was reinforced with the prominent social role played by guilds, confraternities, and pilgrimages in the prayer life of the community, with increasingly important roles assumed by the new orders of friars.[7]

Within this overarching atmosphere of religious nurture, there were distinct developments in specifically catechetical practices. Although the Synod of Albi in 1254 had decreed that children of seven years and over should be brought to so-called religious instruction, there was little said about the specific needs of children.[8] For the adults, the scripture-based *narratio* as expounded by Augustine had gradually given way to a catechetical process centered on the homily at Mass, the recitation of the Creed and the Our Father, and listening to subsequent explanations of these texts. There were concomitant moves to classify knowledge in numerical sets, especially in sets of seven: number of sacraments, deadly sins, and so on.[9] These are signs of a more systematic approach to catechesis inspired, possibly, by the seven petitions of the Lord's Prayer and the seven Beatitudes. In other words, catechesis was organized to facilitate memorization by a largely illiterate people.[10]

The lack of any extant church treatise on the theory and method of catechesis from this time suggests that the Church did not apply its mind specifically to developing this issue. Following the

7 For more on this see Diarmaid MacCulloch, *Reformation: Europe's House Divided 1490–1700* (London: Penguin, 2004) and Lawson, "Learning the Faith in England."

8 Josef Jungmann, "Religious Education in Late Medieval Times," in *Shaping the Christian Message: Essays in Religious Education*, ed. Gerard Sloyan (New York: MacMillan, 1958), 38–62.

9 Jungmann, 40. See also Duffy, *The Stripping of the Altars*, chap. 2.

10 Gerard Sloyan, "Religious Education from Early Christianity to Medieval Times," in Sloyan, *Shaping the Christian Message*, 3–37.

example of the early Church, the liturgical and community life of the Church in the Middle Ages continued, broadly, to serve as the principal formational framework for both children and adults. In this model, children accompanied their parents to religious ceremonies where they absorbed fully the liturgical atmosphere around them. The initial nurturing role of the parents and the wider family was thus assisted by participation in liturgy and an associated Christian community life.[11]

Christian Education as Cultural Renewal

The conversion to Christianity of the northern Frankish tribes and the crowning of Charlemagne (742–814) as Holy Roman Emperor in 800 was a critical moment in the growth of what was to be called "Christendom." Charlemagne sought to renew the continent of Europe through a deepening of Christian culture and belief.[12] The reform of education was at the heart of his ambitious *renovatio*.[13]

The legacy of Augustine's educational "philosophy" underpinned Charlemagne's commitment to enact substantial educational reform.[14] Charlemagne's religiously motivated cultural project sought to restore the "civilization of antiquity" by stressing the importance of education as a culturally unifying force. He was intent on creating a new society that would be grounded in a more educated and literate population.[15] The *renovatio* created the conditions in which the culture of Europe became fully intertwined with Catholic thought. The term

---

11 Cf. Nicholas Orme, *Medieval Schools from Roman Britain to Renaissance England* (New York: Yale University Press, 2006); Evelyn B. Vitz, "Liturgy as Education in the Middle Ages," in *Medieval Education*, ed. Ronald B. Begley and Joseph W. Koterski (New York: Fordham University Press, 2005), 20–34.

12 Hywel Williams, *Emperor of the West: Charlemagne and the Carolingian Empire* (London: Quercus, 2010).

13 Frank P. Graves, *A History of Education Before the Middle Ages* (Hawaii: University Press of the Pacific, 1925/2004).

14 Kevane, *Augustine the Educator*, 113–48.

15 Williams, *Emperor of the West*, 337–42.

"Christendom" hence became an apt description for a continent in which education was the handmaid of the Church.

The reforming energy for the *renovatio* was located in the Christian monasteries, which had evolved over time to become the principal places of Christian education in medieval Europe. These monastic communities were places where Christian life was nurtured by total absorption into the liturgical life and tradition of the Church.[16]

Alongside the celebration of the liturgy, the monastic communities insisted on the frequent and prayerful reading of scripture.[17] Saint Benedict of Nursia (480–547), the founder of western monasticism, had ruled that his monks should spend some time in this spiritual reading (*lectio divina*) every day.[18] In order to provide reading material for the monks, it was essential to gather and copy some of the great texts from across Europe.

The focus on reading necessitated a promotion of literacy among the members of the monastic communities and, by the ninth century, most Benedictine monasteries had a "school" attached, although the pupils were mainly potential members of the monastery. The curriculum in these schools was, broadly speaking, a "liberal arts" education where the study of the Latin and Greek classics, alongside the reading of and meditation on scripture, became the staple diet of the young scholars. Binding it all together was a continuing focus on wisdom as the ultimate goal of education.[19] The continued emphasis on the value of the liberal arts as pathways to the contemplation of the divine allowed the later medieval mind to see the ordering of all knowledge as a way of glimpsing the hand of God in all things.

16 Marilyn Dunn, *The Emergence of Monasticism* (Oxford: Blackwell, 2000).

17 Learning to read in medieval times was chiefly, but not exclusively, accomplished in ecclesiastical foundations. See Williams, *Emperor of the West*, 338–39.

18 Benedict, *The Rule of St. Benedict in English* (Collegeville, MN: The Liturgical Press, 1982), chap. 48.

19 Hugo of St. Victor, *Didascalion*, trans. Jerome Taylor (New York: Columbia University Press, 12th century/1961).

More broadly, these developments were woven throughout a related concatenation of social and educational initiatives beginning with the rise of the cathedral schools and the emergence of the European universities in the second millennium of Christianity.[20] The universities played a major role in the upcoming intellectual controversy over Scholasticism, which would leave a profound mark on Catholic thought. The Church, which had been the determinative source of influence in medieval Europe, soon had to respond to significant intellectual challenges from other ways of thinking.

The Influence of
Wider Intellectual Movements on Catechesis

The encounter between Christianity and the Muslim empire, which had expanded across Europe in the late medieval period, was another landmark event in church history. The consequent "rediscovery" of the Aristotelian *corpus,* and the ensuing debate on the place of Aristotelianism in Christian thought (the so-called Scholastic Debate) was a key moment in the emergence of more educational aspects of formation.[21]

Scholasticism as such was an educational method which sought to show the interrelatedness of all Christian doctrine and how this body of teaching was in accord with reason. Hence, clerical training in the "schools" was instrumental in reforming religious instruction for converts according to Scholastic lines. Although there is some consonance between this debate and the similar debate over the place of Greek thought in early Christianity, the (perceived) medieval

---

20 James Bowen, *A History of Western Education*, vol. 2, *Civilization of Europe, Sixth to Sixteenth Century* (London: Methuen, 1975), chap. 2.

21 There is an abundance of valuable material on these epochal developments, some more accessible than others to the nonspecialist. See, for example, Aidan Nichols, *Discovering Aquinas* (London: Darton, Longman, and Todd, 2002) and "Thomas Aquinas," *Stanford Encyclopedia of Philosophy* (2022), https://plato.stanford.edu/entries/aquinas/.

conflict between reason and authority took matters in a new direction as it seemed to sow seeds of division between learning and the Christian foundations of medieval society.

The work of Thomas Aquinas (1225–1274) epitomized the Christian position vis-à-vis faith and reason. Western (or Latin) Christianity became increasingly underpinned by his pioneering synthesis of faith and reason, which had a profound influence on the educational thought of the time.[22] Aquinas's focus on the God-given place of reason in the broader educational process thus offered a new perspective on the Augustinian vision of education.[23] Moreover, while Aquinas accepted the concept of learning by discovery, he also emphasized the need to learn by formal instruction. This was a significant move toward an approach to learning in which the role of the teacher was that of "instructor" as well as "facilitator."[24]

Aquinas was writing in a cultural context in which attitudes toward children veered between models rooted in the so-called "depravity" or "innocence" of children and the related uniqueness of the experiences of the child.[25] This cultural interplay casts a fresh light on the claim that Aquinas was the first to provide a theological rationale for a so-called developmental model of childhood.[26] While verification of these claims requires further study, his *Catechetical Instructions* offer glimpses of a twofold approach involving both faith and reason. For example, in discussing the fourth commandment, Aquinas mentioned the duty of parents to form their children religiously "without

22 Dennis Doyle, "Integrating Faith and Reason in the Catholic School," *Catholic Education: A Journal of Inquiry and Practice* 10, no. 3 (2007): 343–56.

23 T. Brian Mooney and Mark Nowacki, eds., *Understanding Teaching and Learning: Classic Texts on Education by Augustine, Aquinas, Newman and Mill* (Exeter: Imprint Academic, 2011).

24 Thomas Aquinas, *On Truth*, vol. 2, *Questions X-XX*, trans, James V. McGlynn (Cambridge: Hackett, 1994), question 11.

25 Robert A. Davis, "Brilliance of a Fire: Innocence, Experience and the Theory of Childhood," *Journal of Philosophy of Education* 45, no. 2 (2011): 379–97.

26 Cristina Traina, "A Person in the Making: Thomas Aquinas on Children and Childhood," in Bunge, *The Child in Christian Thought*, 103–33.

delay," as part of their threefold gift to their children of "birth, nourishment and instruction."[27] Nourishment refers in the first place to physical care, but it also infers a nurture approach to education that complements the instruction he recommended. This synthesis between nurture and instruction in the rearing of children, with a clear awareness of the value of an intellectual diet (for adults) in the liberal arts, is a further and significant development of catechetical processes. The importance of cultivating reason was now increasingly fused with the catechetical paradigm.[28]

Scholasticism, however, came under critical scrutiny in the late medieval period from the variegated social and cultural movement known as "humanism." The use of the term "humanism" can be problematic owing to contemporary understandings of humanism as a school of thought that denies the relevance or existence of God.[29] Nonetheless, it is this *classical* humanism that links the early Middle Ages with the Renaissance and the Enlightenment.[30]

Humanism promoted a cultural rebirth (*il rinascimento / le rennaissance*) in which classical texts were studied in the original languages. More importantly, these texts were deemed worthy of study in their own right and not just as adumbrations of the beliefs of Christianity and/or its ethical code. In northern Europe this attachment to classical texts was translated into a religious movement that sought to reassess Christian thought in the light of history.[31]

---

27 Thomas Aquinas, *The Catechetical Instructions of St. Thomas Aquinas,* trans. Joseph B. Collins (Manila: Sinag-Tala, 13th century/1939).

28 Aquinas's contemporary Saint Bonaventure (1221–1274) also argued for the place of reason in Catholic thinking.

29 See Appendix I for some initial thoughts on Christian humanism in the *Global Compact on Education* established by Pope Francis in 2019.

30 For more on the Catholic contribution to "enlightened" thinking, see Ulrich Lehner, *The Catholic Enlightenment: The Forgotten History of a Global Movement* (Oxford: Oxford University Press, 2016).

31 Once again there is a plethora of material seeking to illuminate this historical moment. See Erika Rummell, *Erasmus* (London: Continuum Books, 2004) and István Bejczy, *Erasmus and the Middle Ages* (Leiden: Brill, 2001).

In essence, Christian humanists sought to reestablish the connection between the perceived simple message of the Gospels and the daily life of the believer. In their eyes, the Scholastic focus on philosophical method had fractured this relationship. This could only be healed, it was claimed, by a return to the study of the Gospels (*ad fontes*) in the original language.

The influence of Christian humanism was exemplified by a Dutch religious order/movement, The Brethren of the Common Life, whose focus was education in Christian humanist ways of thinking and living. The movement was initiated by Gerard de Groote (1340–1384). It used the classical educational tools of the liberal arts curriculum to study scripture and find therein the true message of Jesus which, they claimed, had been obscured by many accretions and human traditions.[32] From this movement there emerged the *devotio moderna* school which, recalling some aspects of the early Christian opposition to dialogue with Greek philosophy, argued that intense study of nonspiritual matters was damaging to a Christian's faith life.[33]

Two works illustrate the influence of this thinking on Catholic spirituality. *The Imitation of Christ* by Thomas à Kempis (c.1379–1471) is perhaps the most famous book to emerge from the *devotio moderna* school, although its intended audience was principally those in the monastic life, not young people. The question of catechesis for children was addressed by Jean Gerson (1363–1429) in *On Leading Children to Christ*.[34] This tract is located clearly within the catechetical paradigm and is an application of the principles of the *devotio moderna* to children's catechesis. In response to critics who thought that the

---

32 This movement seems to prefigure trends in scholarship in the nineteenth and twentieth centuries related to the search for the "historical Jesus" as opposed to the "Christ of faith."

33 "Woe to them that inquire of men after many curious things and are little curious of the way to serve me." Thomas à Kempis, *My Imitation of Christ* (Brooklyn: Confraternity of the Precious Blood, 1954), chap. 43. This is an example of the principles underlying the *devotio moderna.*

34 This important text is found in Kendig B. Cully, ed., *Basic Writings in Christian Education* (Philadelphia: Westminster, 1960).

teaching of children was beneath his dignity as a university professor in Paris, Gerson saw his work with children as being of equal status to the study of deeper theological issues.[35] Yet a closer reading of his argument suggests that Gerson's preferred model of childhood is not too clear. On the one hand, the child is seen as a delicate plant who needs protection from evil influences. This suggests that Gerson is influenced by the childhood model of so-called religious innocence. On the other hand, Gerson is clear that young children need regular confession owing to their sinful state. In this latter statement, it is not clear if he is referring to a specific group of young people or is making a broader theological statement about children as a whole.

What is noteworthy here is the importance placed by Gerson on the spiritual direction of children by means of the sacrament of confession and his stress on the need to teach and guide children with love—although this does not exclude direct instruction in doctrine.[36] It is, in short, an example of the need to include children in the wider catechetical processes and to offer them concrete spiritual direction.

The range of catechetical and educational developments in the medieval period offers a set of signposts for the argument of the present book. While there is little doubt that the catechetical paradigm remains predominant, what emerges is the growing influence of broader educational initiatives rooted in the desire to nurture Christian faith. The end of the medieval period was a crucial time for the Church as the internal clamor for broader and deeper church reform was growing stronger throughout Europe. There were other significant geopolitical and theological contours to this historical era, the treatment of which are beyond the immediate scope of the present book. These were crystallized in the Protestant Reformation and the Catholic Reform movements, both of which radically altered the shape of early modern Christianity. The influence of the latter on catechesis will be examined in the third historical context.

---

35 Brian P. McGuire, *Jean Gerson and the Last Medieval Reformation* (Philadelphia: University of Pennsylvania Press, 2005).

36 Sloyan, "Religious Education," in Sloyan, *Shaping the Christian Message*, 34–36.

CHAPTER 3

THE CATHOLIC REFORM
AND CATECHESIS

The Catholic Reform and Catechesis, the third historical context, explores how the Council of Trent (1545–1563) reaffirmed the principles of Catholic thought in the face of opposition from the Reformed Christian communities of Europe. The key reforms set in motion by the council prepared the ground for the rise of religious orders and congregations dedicated to education. This provided the foundational blocks for modern educational structures and curricula.

In early modern Europe, population pressure, pandemics, the rise of the cities, and the rediscovery of the achievements of classical antiquity all contributed to an atmosphere of intellectual and cultural ferment, leading to the eventual dissolution of the medieval order. The moves to reform the Church from within, as well as dealing with external challenges, are a further reflection of a powerful narrative of change and continuity.

The Catholic reform substantially strengthened the inherited catechetical paradigm of religious education. The Tridentine Church drew heavily on its own resources, especially Scholastic methods, in order to respond in a resilient manner to the doctrinal and educational challenges it faced from the reformers.

34

The Council of Trent and Catechesis

The Council of Trent was the foremost component of the Catholic reform. Trent sought to reform many of the abuses that had taken root in the Church in the two centuries since the Black Death (1346–1353).[1] It promoted unity of faith and defined the key points of Catholic doctrine in the face of opposition from the reformers. The council's tools were the Vulgate Bible, the Roman (Tridentine) liturgy, the Code of Canon Law, and the Roman Catechism.

The Council of Trent saw education as the vital force in the Church's ongoing internal reform. There were two aspects to this. First, and in response to the reformers' desire to use education and schooling as a driver for ecclesial and societal reform, the Catholic Church recognized the necessity of fostering the printed word via printing presses and the construction of ecclesiastical libraries— these were visible manifestation of their prized inherited tradition. Second, and in response to the reformers' successful focus on the preaching of the Word of God, the art of preaching was given renewed emphasis as a method of catechesis.[2] In the Catholic Church, preaching had been traditionally reserved to members of (certain) religious orders. But now the onus was placed on parish priests. This timely shift required suitable preparation of priests and those intending to become priests.

To achieve this laudable goal, a form of higher education was established for young men preparing for priesthood.[3] The founding of seminaries was a key moment of the Catholic reform and recognized the comparatively poor state of clerical preaching and, indeed, the apparent deficiencies in the broader cultural and intellectual formation of parish priests throughout the Catholic Church. The

1 Joseph Byrne, *The Black Death* (Westport, CT: Greenwood, 2004).

2 MacCulloch, *Reformation: Europe's House Divided*, 280–303.

3 Particular emphasis was put on the doctrine of the Eucharist. See, for example, Council of Trent, session 23, "Decree Concerning the Doctrine of the Eucharist," *Canons and Decrees of the Council of Trent*, trans. Henry J. Schroeder (Rockford, IL: Tan Books, 1978), 72–87.

seminaries brought together academic studies and a life of piety in a single institution; this was an important indicator of the merging of catechetical and educational paradigms of religious formation. As these seminaries were under the direction of the diocesan bishop, and not part of the network of universities, the link with the pastoral theme of religious nurture was inevitably highlighted.

Alongside the new initiatives in the formation of seminarians, the Council of Trent aimed to develop the knowledge and skills of the existing corps of parish priests. It proposed that on Sundays and on the principal feasts of the liturgical year, the bishop and parish priests would catechize the congregations in a manner suitable to the capacity of the audience.[4] It is worth noting that the needs of children were specifically recognized in these directives, although without precise details of how this could be done.[5] This seems to be in keeping with the medieval emphasis on the inclusion of the child within the broader catechesis undertaken by the wider community.

In broad terms, the liturgical year would serve as a leitmotif for this demanding enterprise of catechetical preaching. The devotional life of the Church would, ostensibly, provide the material for a more scholastic input into preaching and teaching. Such linking of worship and teaching recalled the teaching mission of the first believers as recounted in the New Testament. What is significant in the Tridentine age is the development of the earlier focus on community and liturgical life, aiming toward a more formal and systematic approach. All of this is centered on the priesthood and preaching and, with the support of groups like the Confraternity of Christian Doctrine, the

---

4   The clergy "shall at least on Sundays and solemn festivals either personally, or if they are lawfully impeded, through others who are competent, feed the people committed to them with wholesome words in proportion to their own and their people's mental capacity." Council of Trent, session 5, chap. 2, "On Preaching," in *Canons and Decrees of the Council of Trent*, 26.

5   "The Bishops shall also see to it that at least on Sunday and other festival days, the children in every parish be carefully taught the rudiments of the faith and obedience toward God and their parents." Council of Trent, session 24, chap. 4, "Decree Concerning Reform," in *Canons and Decrees of the Council of Trent*, 196.

use of printed catechisms. Nonetheless, we need to ask whether the Tridentine emphasis on catechisms diminished the importance of the life of the church community as a formative force. The Jesuit scholar and twentieth-century catechetical reformer Joseph Jungmann (1889–1975) has argued that the focus on the written word of the texts and catechisms detracted from liturgy and art as instruments of education.[6] Clearly, the Church sought to counter the effects of the Reformation by adopting methods that the reformers themselves were adopting in their mission to rebuild the Church. Regardless of how we address the concern raised by Jungmann, the historical evidence shows that the community dimension remained at the heart of the catechetical process. It was given renewed vitality by the Council of Trent, which encouraged religious instruction in the vernacular tongue and addressed the differing needs of the members of community.[7]

The Roman Catechism and Catechesis

The sixteenth century saw a major development in catechesis with the publication in 1529 of Martin Luther's *Catechism*. While catechesis had traditionally operated in preparation for Christian initiation, and was marked historically by active participation in liturgical and the community life of the Church, the advent of the printed catechism

---

6 Josef Jungmann, *Handing on the Faith*, trans. A. N. Fuerst (London: Burns and Oates, 1965). See context in chap. 4 below.

7   That the faithful may approach the sacraments with greater reverence and devotion of mind, the holy council commands all bishops that not only when they shall first, in a manner adapted to the mental ability of those who receive them, explain their efficacy and use, but also they shall see to it that the same is done piously and prudently by every parish priest, and in the vernacular tongue, if need be and it can be done conveniently, in accordance with the form which will be prescribed for each of the sacraments by the holy council in a catechism which the bishops shall have faithfully translated into the language of the people and explained to the people by all parish priests." (Council of Trent, session 24, chap. 7, "Decree Concerning Reform," in *Canons and Decrees of the Council of Trent*, 197).

reconfigured this tradition by formally setting out key doctrines in a question and answer format. The invention of printing allowed the resultant texts to have a wide circulation and the use of catechisms became a distinctive and significant feature of catechesis from the middle of the sixteenth century onward.[8]

The reformers' defining desire to promote a "'priesthood of all believers'"[demanded a (reformed) church population with the literacy skills needed to have access to the Bible in the vernacular. Interestingly, the Tridentine Catholic Church took up Luther's idea that catechesis should be rooted in a written, detailed account of Christian doctrine.

The systematic organization of knowledge exemplified in the genre of catechism recalled the structure of the medieval encyclopedia. But now this knowledge base was rooted in Christian doctrine with an explicitly apologetic, or confessional, focus.

This process (or system) had its origins in earlier forms of instruction following the Byzantine methods of *erotapokriseis* (question-and-answer) and dialogue.[9] The Roman Catechism, however, published in 1566, adopted a discursive, not question-and-answer, style and thus facilitated the further development of the catechism as a specific genre of religious and educational literature alongside its original meaning as a process of Christian instruction.

The aim of the Roman Catechism, as stated in its preface, was to offer a conspectus of the Catholic theological tradition in the context of broader spiritual development. Significantly, the Roman Catechism offered clear direction on teaching methodology. In keeping with the approach of the canons and decrees of the Council of Trent on preaching and teaching, it recommended a differentiation

8 John O'Malley, *The First Jesuits* (Cambridge, MA: Harvard University Press, 1993).

9 Yannis Papadoyannakis, "Instruction by Question and Answer: The Case of Late Antique and Byzantine Erotapokriseis," in *Greek Literature in Late Antiquity: Dynamism, Didacticism, Classicism*, ed. S. Fitzgerald Johnson (Aldershot, UK: Ashgate, 2006), 91–106.

according to age and capacity.[10] This is another important sign of an increasingly sophisticated understanding of how catechesis should be developed.

This guide to methodology is a reminder that the Roman Catechism was not intended for a wide readership. Its primary audience was parish priests: this group of men was charged with improving the quality of their preaching and instruction by ensuring that they were aware of the theological foundations of the Catholic faith. In a sense, this is an early example of what is now called ongoing "professional development" for teachers: a timely recognition that all teachers (parish priests were also teachers/catechists) need to update their knowledge base. Hence the Roman Catechism could be described as one of the first teacher's manuals in education, incorporating material for a structured and detailed curriculum to be adapted according to the needs of the audience.

Given the attention to broader methodological principles enunciated by the Council of Trent, there arose the opportunity to consider how catechisms designed specifically for children could enhance their religious formation.[11] One example of this catechetical energy was the triple catechism of Saint Peter Canisius (1521–1597), published around 1555–1558 (before the Roman Catechism) and, significantly, with three parts aimed at young children, adolescents, and young adults. The explicit differentiation of content recognized the developmental needs of young people and their place in the life of a teaching Church. This is a significant indicator that the Catholic Church was responding positively to educational reforms in other Christian communities.

The Roman Catechism's systematic exposition of doctrine was a clear strength, albeit with some limitations. First, its linkage of

---

10 The Council of Trent refers to the necessity of differentiation: "Age, capacity, manners and condition demand attention, that he who instructs may become all things to all men, and be able to gain all to Christ." Preface to the *Catechism of the Council of Trent.*

11 Council of Trent, session 24, chap. 7, "Decree Concerning Reform."

catechesis with theology laid open the danger of reducing the study of theology to a textbook exercise at arm's length from liturgy and worship. Second, it was not clear if a more doctrinally focused study of scripture would impinge upon a prayerful reading of the sacred texts in a broader program of studies centered on the Roman Catechism. Finally, the textbook approach, along with the move to classroom or "Sunday School"–style instruction driven by the Confraternity of Christian Doctrine, suggests that the study of Christianity was in danger of becoming a largely cognitive exercise separate from the pastoral life of the worshipping Church. This final point is what underpinned the critical historical work of Joseph Jungmann in the twentieth century.

These important issues notwithstanding, the importance of the Roman Catechism in the history of catechesis should not be minimized. It exemplified a clear progression from the medieval community's approach. It retained the four traditional catechetical pillars of creed, sacraments, moral life, and prayer and successfully incorporated these components into a format designed to counter the doctrinal and structural challenges posed by the Protestant Reformation. A more systematic and scholastic conceptualization of catechesis was developed from this base during the following centuries.

Post-Tridentine Catechesis and the School

In the turbulent years of late sixteenth-century Europe, the Catholic Church and the communities emerging from the Protestant Reformation sought to use education as a key force in their ongoing religious and cultural debates.

The interplay between catechesis and education at this time was strengthened considerably by the gradual migration of catechesis to Catholic schools. The Catholic Church's catechetical methods at this time developed the inherited traditions and, in the light of the Tridentine reforms, continued the systematization of catechesis alongside the development of broader reforms in education and schooling.

In the centuries after the Reformation, there was an explosion of Catholic religious orders and congregations with a charism for education.[12] The work of the Society of Jesus (the Jesuits) and the De La Salle Brothers, for example, reflected the Church's conviction that its growing network of schools would be loci of catechesis. Indeed, such Catholic educational enterprises were the vital link between the education offered by the monasteries / cathedral schools of the Middle Ages and the mass education of the nineteenth century. They continued the reforms in education which, although predating the events of the Reformation, were given renewed impetus by the energy arising from the Catholic Reform. It is here that we find the roots of the modern curriculum, the importance given to the printed word in both textbooks and teachers' manuals, and the origin of the formation of educators.

The post-Tridentine catechetical and educational reforms were driven by the Society of Jesus.[13] Their influence on education in general rests on their claimed integration of faith and learning.[14] The Jesuits saw their mission as one of correcting the post-Reformation doctrinal confusion by the building of an integrated intellectual and pastoral culture in their growing network of schools. The Jesuits reconfigured the doctrinal heritage of Catholicism into a lasting educational apostolate. This focus on doctrinal orthodoxy within an

---

12   Cf. Tom O'Donoghue, *Catholic Teaching Brothers: Their Life in the English-Speaking World 1891–1965* (New York: Palgrave Macmillan, 2012); Ronnie Po-chia Hsia, *The World of Catholic Renewal 1540–1770* (Cambridge: Cambridge University Press, 2005); Bart Hellinckx, Frank Simon, and Marc Depaepe, *The Forgotten Contribution of the Teaching Sisters* (Leuven: Leuven University Press, 2009).

13   For more on this, see Aldo D. Scaglione, *The Liberal Arts and the Jesuit College System* (Amsterdam: John Benjamins, 1986).

14   Although the Jesuits are not a *product* of the Council of Trent, they were caught up in the general wave of reform that permeated the Catholic world at this time. The formation of Jesuit priests, based on the *Spiritual Exercises* of Ignatius allied to a solid theological education, was without precedent in religious life at the time. They had thus responded to the Tridentine call for better-formed clergy. Within a very short time, they had become the most influential Catholic order in education.

educational context is evidence of one cohesive paradigm of Christian education that is simultaneously catechetical and educational.

The Jesuit blend of theology and intellectualism covered elementary, secondary, and tertiary education.[15] In the Ratio Studiorum, the Jesuits set out their vision of an educational system centered on four areas: administration, curriculum, method, and discipline.[16] The focus in the Ratio Studiorum on the links between cognitive learning and the development of good habits suggests that the Jesuit vision of education was a groundbreaking attempt to marry the best of Scholasticism and Christian humanism. The Jesuit vision was subsequently enlarged in the educational thought of Giambattista Vico (1668–1744) who, in opposition to the predominance of Cartesian logic in education, reasserted more ancient and abiding forms of the philosophical life rooted in the attachment to instinct, custom, tradition, myth, community, piety, and faith.[17]

The innovative pedagogy of the Jesuits was centered on a systematic and progressive arrangement of subjects to be taught. In particular, they advocated the practice of an introductory overview/ mapping of the subject matter related to a particular issue before moving on to a more detailed study of individual components and topics. It is reasonable to infer that specific catechetical classes would have adopted this method. If so, there are clear parallels with the early Christian *narratio* in which the events of salvation history were

---

15 David Hamilton, *Towards a Theory of Schooling* (East Sussex: The Falmer Press, 1989).

16 This complemented the scope of the Roman Catechism—while the Roman Catechism set out the religious curriculum as a teaching handbook for priests, the Ratio Studiorum offered a broader vision of education that encompassed the wider field of studies and amalgamated a number of earlier documents on education by Jesuit thinkers. In fact, the Ratio Studiorum was nothing less than a handbook for a complete educational system. For a tabulated analysis of the Ratio, see John Padberg, "Development of the *Ratio Studiorum*" in *The Jesuit Ratio Studiorum: 400th Anniversary Perspectives*, ed. Vincent Duminuco (New York: Fordham University Press, 2000), 99.

17 Robert A. Davis, "Giambattista Vico and the Wisdom of Teaching," *Asia Pacific Review* 15, no. 1 (2014): 45–33.

presented to the catechumens as part of their gradual journey of initiation. By the post-Reformation period, doctrine—as presented in the key formulae found in various catechisms—formed a new *narratio* that succeeded the Augustinian story-method.

Educational method and the organization of schools were also key concerns of John Baptiste de La Salle (1651–1719). In common with the Jesuits, de La Salle's vision of education, as set out in his famous work, *The Conduct of Schools,* was an expression of pastoral theology geared toward the spiritual and human needs of pupils.[18] For example, de La Salle was revolutionary in his vetoing of the use of Latin in favor of the vernacular as the language of instruction—he believed that a knowledge of French would aid his pupils' future spiritual growth by enabling them to read a wider selection of Christian doctrine when they left school.[19] Furthermore, de La Salle favored a more cooperative and collaborative methodology in the classrooms of his schools. In catechism classes, for example, the teacher is directed not to speak to the pupils except by way of direct or indirect questions in order to assist their comprehension. De La Salle was keen to avoid a narrow focus on doctrinal tenets bereft of a solid pastoral support system within a Catholic community of learners.

De La Salle's work was a crucial step in the development of a school-based catechesis owing to the emphasis he placed on ordered learning in all subjects. The desire to promote an ordered and pastoral learning environment required a corps of suitably formed teachers.[20] Where the Council of Trent had established seminaries for future priests, de La Salle pioneered the spread of

---

18 Carl Koch, Jeffrey Calligan, and Jeffrey Gros, eds., *John Baptiste de la Salle: The Spirituality of Christian Education* (New Jersey: Paulist Press, 2004). For a classic account of de La Salle's place in the history of pedagogy, see Gabriel Compayré, *The History of Pedagogy,* trans. W.H Payne (London: Bloomsbury, 1905).

19 Koch, Calligan, and Gros, *John Baptiste de la Salle,* 128.

20 A case could be made that school teachers and parish priests were the primary agents of the Counter-Reformation in France at this time. See Karen Carter, *Creating Catholics: Catechism and Primary Education in Early Modern France* (Notre Dame, IN: University of Notre Dame Press, 2012), 137f.

educational centers dedicated to the training of lay teachers in doctrinal orthodoxy and general pastoral care. This challenged the link between the priest and the catechetical processes that Trent had firmly established, complemented the Tridentine emphasis on the formation of seminarians, and, crucially, recognized the importance of the (lay) educator in the broader life of the Church. De La Salle's initiative anticipated the Second Vatican Council's promotion of the universal call to holiness and the later related emphasis on the distinctive vocation of the lay Catholic teacher.[21] This bypassing of the universities as a locus for the "training" of teachers may suggest that he regarded an overly cognitive approach to the formation of educators as insufficiently pastoral in intent. What is beyond doubt is that de La Salle was offering an innovative perspective on how prospective teachers should be formed.

The Catholic Reform brought together disparate religious practices to form a detailed code of practice centered on the geographical structure of the single parochial channel of the diocese, with prominent roles afforded to the parish priest and bishop.[22] There is once again no sense of a division between catechesis and religious education. The confessionalization of post-Tridentine catechesis reflected the doctrinal divisions in Christianity but there was little or no questioning of the need for religious faith. This would soon change as new ideas originating in the period now known as the Enlightenment about the validity of the religious experience of humanity would challenge the whole spectrum of Christianity.

---

21 *Lay Catholics in Schools*, 1982.
22 John Bossy, "The Counter-Reformation and the People of Catholic Europe." in *The Counter-Reformation*, ed. David Luebke (Oxford: Blackwell, 1999), 85–104.

CHAPTER 4

THE CATECHETICAL RENEWAL
OF THE EARLY TWENTIETH CENTURY

The Catechetical Renewal of the Early Twentieth Century, the fourth historical context, saw increased demands for reform in Catholic thinking about catechesis as well as about areas like scripture and liturgy. This multipronged movement drew on the emerging field of educational research and was a crucial moment in the Church's ongoing reform. It prepared the ground for the Church's educational reforms that came to prominence in the final quarter of the twentieth century.

In the years following the Reformation, both Catholic and Reformed thinkers, although separated in key aspects of Christian doctrine, were component parts of a society that recognized the importance of religion. This arrangement was challenged when the new ideas arising from the Enlightenment and the French Revolution (1787–1799) questioned the continuing predominance of the Christian intellectual and philosophical heritage.[1] Significantly, many Enlightenment thinkers saw education as the key driver of the people's liberation from the perceived restraints of revealed religion.[2]

---

1 Roy Porter, *The Enlightenment* (Hampshire, UK: Palgrave, 2001).
2 Anthony Podgen, *The Enlightenment and Why It Still Matters* (Oxford: Oxford University Press, 2013).

By the late nineteenth and early twentieth centuries there was, in consequence, a complex and difficult relationship between the Church and the broader cultural climate.[3] Within this fervent intellectual atmosphere, catechesis continued to evolve according to the catechetical and educational paradigms that the Tridentine reforms had inherited from previous centuries. The catechetical and educational paradigms of religious education were hence fully part of the critical reforms in church life that took place at this time.

The catechetical movement's focus on the reform of catechetical method was the fruit of a dialogue with broader thinking in education. This option for reform served to strengthen the educational paradigm of religious education. Furthermore, the catechetical movement's focus on reform of the content of catechesis was an attempt to balance the earlier educationally inspired reforms and foster the catechetical paradigm in the light of advances in liturgical and scriptural scholarship.

The Early Catechetical Movement:
The Focus on Method

The determination of the Church to retain catechesis in the school was predicated on an understandable desire to use the classroom as the principal means of halting the perceived de-Christianization of society set in motion by the Enlightenment and associated ways of thinking.[4] The school, and more precisely the elementary (primary) school, is where the competing forces of Church, society, and the modern state struggled for supremacy.

By virtue of the mass schooling that arose from urbanization and industrialization, the catechesis of children at the end of the nineteenth century had become, in the main, a school-based activity.

3 Pope Pius X, Encyclical Letter *Pascendi Dominici Gregis* (1907).
4 It is not the case, however, that the Enlightenment period was universally hostile to religion. There were "enlightened" Catholics who sought engagement with new thinking. For more on this, see Lehner, *The Catholic Enlightenment: The Forgotten History of a Global Movement* (2016).

It should not be forgotten that the loss of community ritual, itself a doleful consequence of the phenomenon of urbanization, was a key element in the desire of the schools to serve as points of reference for a Catholic population that had been largely displaced from its inherited network of rural religious traditions.

There were certainly many positive aspects to this school-based catechesis, most notably the integral formation that arose from having catechetical classes alongside other subjects according to an ordered timetable. More problematic was the continued use of theological categories arising from Scholastic philosophical and theological frameworks with children. When allied to the prevailing use of the Roman Catechism and other catechisms as texts to be memorized, this amalgam of methods was less than effective for proclaiming the Gospel in a time of intellectual and educational reform.

Against this backdrop, new ideas for reforming catechesis circulated in Europe, especially in Germany. These ideas were influenced in part by the work of the educational theorist Johann Herbart (1776–1841), who had emphasized the importance of methodology and, in particular, the role of the teacher, in the teaching-learning process. His key point of emphasis was the vital importance of the lesson plan in education—this platform was where the teacher, from a position of knowledge, set out how to mold the child, control behavior, and develop learning.[5]

We must bear in mind that the first stage of the catechetical reform was solely a reform of method based on the findings of wider educational research. The early catechetical reformers took the existing catechetical practice—based largely on memorization of the catechism—and applied Herbartian ideas to it.[6] The results of this reform was a revised catechetical method based on a three-step

---

5   An overview of the Herbartian approach is found in Bowen, *A History of Western Education*, vol. 3 (London: Methuen, 1981), 232–41.

6   This involved a lesson plan–based approach that began with Scripture followed by "text-explanatio," usually directed by the catechist/teacher. It ended with the use of the catechism to explain the point of doctrine set out in the lesson plan.

process of *presentation, explanation,* and *application.*[7] This set the stage for the use of planning sheets that allowed the teacher to show in advance how a set of lessons would be developed.

The interplay between catechesis and educational psychology provides important evidence of dialogue between the Church and wider learning in a period when such exchanges were often viewed suspiciously.[8] There was some attempt to move away from a purely cognitive approach to learning by engaging with the reality of daily life in the application stage of the lesson. However, this method-reform movement did little to challenge the doctrinal framework of the catechetical sessions. It continued to emphasize the role of story in catechesis, itself a faint echo of the *narratio* of the early Church. On the whole, the reforms failed to address in any depth issues arising from the intrusion the language of Scholastic theology in a process designed to foster the faith of children. Should I cite in a footnote the book on Shields here?

An example of the dialogue with educational psychology is the application of the "age of reason" debate to the celebration of the ceremony of First Holy Communion.[9] This is seen in the directive *Quam Singulari,* issued under Pope Pius X's authority on August 8, 1910.[10] Pius was keen to dispel the view that Holy Communion was a reward for goodness and virtue instead of the principal means to achieve these ends. For this reason, he allowed young children access to the sacrament of Holy Communion before they had demonstrated a "full and perfect knowledge of Christian doctrine," while reminding the Church that "the child will be obliged to learn gradually the entire catechism according to his ability." From this evidence, the place of

---

7   The three-stage method corresponded to the broader Herbartian approach. For more on this, see Berard Marthaler, "The Modern Catechetical Movement in Roman Catholicism: Issues and Personalities," *Religious Education* 73, no. 5, supp. 1 (1978): 77–91.

8   Pius X, *Pascendi Dominici Gregis.*

9   This issue is explored in Peter McGrail, *First Communion Ritual, Church and Popular Religious Identity* (Aldershot, UK: Ashgate, 2007), 13, 38.

10 Sacred Congregation of the Discipline of the Sacraments, *Quam Singulari* (1910).

the Roman Catechism in catechesis was not up for debate. Yet there was still a recognized need for differentiation according to aptitude and development. Crucially, the reforms to First Communion enacted by Pius X are another indication of the modest reform of the catechetical paradigm in the light of dialogue with other thinking. It suggests a more accommodating approach to new ideas than is evident in his robustly anti-Modernist encyclical, *Pascendi,* published in 1907.

In summary, the early stages of the twentieth-century catechetical reform evolved in response to dialogue with other disciplines, especially educational psychology. While the radical edge of the early catechetical movement was highlighted in its adaptation of Herbartian pedagogy, this radicalism did not yet include a marked sense of the need to reform the content of catechesis. Soon, the second stage of the catechetical renewal would develop a more precise connection between the related liturgical and catechetical movements. This would be concretized principally in the work of the Jesuit priest, Josef Jungmann.

The Early Catechetical Movement: The Focus on Content

By the 1930s there was a change in perspective with regard to the development of catechesis. This second stage of the reform sought to refocus on the perceived joy of the Gospel, which had been lost, it was claimed, amidst the learning of layers of theological formulae derived from the Roman Catechism. At the heart of this second stage of reform was the strengthening of the links between catechetical renewal and other reform movements in the Church, especially the liturgical movement. Religious education was understood as the continuing proclamation of the Good News of salvation (*kerygma*) which would, somehow, elicit the response of good living from its subjects.

The key figure of this movement is Josef Jungmann, whose work is best understood as an attempt to reclaim the nurturing heart of catechesis from the perceived arid Scholastic approaches underpinning post-Tridentine methods. At the heart of Jungmann's theology is the intervention of grace within the life of the Church. His endeavors to reimagine catechesis in this light are reflected in two important works: *The Good News Yesterday and Today*, published in 1962, and *Handing on the Faith*, published in 1965.[11] Jungmann recognized the aims and objectives of the early reforms to method but felt that the perceived disproportionate focus on the effective presentation of content skirted the key challenge then facing the Church's catechetical work: the lack of an appreciation of the concept of salvation history rooted in knowing, celebrating, and living the *kerygma* "in all its beauty and in all its supernatural sublimity."[12]

Jungmann objected to the intrusion of largely cognitive approaches to learning in what, he insisted, should be a process of religious proclamation, driven by grace and rooted in the vibrant liturgical life of the Christian community. Such cognitive approaches to catechesis, inspired in part by the Tridentine settlement and contextualized in the polarized religious atmosphere of late sixteenth-century Europe and beyond, were, in Jungmann's eyes, an unwelcome imposition of theology and its associated language and methodology onto the catechesis of the young. As a corrective to the perceived dominance of what he saw as the abstract language and intellectual processes of theology in catechesis, Jungmann sought inspiration in a somewhat idealized vision of the early Church, which had, he claimed, exhibited a "pristine spirit and single-mindedness of its Christian life and in the clarity of its ideals."[13]

---

11 Josef Jungmann, *The Good News Yesterday and Today* (New York: W. H. Sadlier, 1962). This text was initially published in the late 1930s but did not make a significant impact on the life of the Church until after the Second Vatican Council.

12 Jungmann, *Handing on the Faith*, 36.

13 Jungmann, *The Good News Yesterday and Today*, 17. This approach reflected the late medieval humanists' desire to return *"ad fonte"* as part of a renaissance of interest in early Christianity. Jungmann was in effect adopting the same hermeneutic as the humanists.

Jungmann proposed strengthening the existing systematic methods of catechesis with a wider vision designed to proclaim the joy (*kerygma*) of the Gospel. For example, he saw the liturgical year as a complete course in Christian teaching that presented afresh, through its succession of liturgical feasts, all the key moments of salvation history. This appreciation of the Gospel message would provide a cultural challenge to Christians whose spiritual life, both personal and corporate, owed more to local customs and a burdensome list of poorly understood obligations.

Jungmann incorporated the vision of the liturgical movement into his catechetical work in order to provide an initial synthesis of reform-minded developments. The proclamation of the Christian message could not, therefore, be separated from the liturgy. Such a primary focus on the liturgy enhanced Jungmann's position as a key advocate of a catechetical paradigm of religious education.[14]

Certain limitations arise from Jungmann's approach, despite its initial appeal. First, the apparent focus on catechesis as an activity primarily for children sits uneasily with the early Church's focus on adult conversion. More important, however, is the emphasis on the liturgy as means of formation. Although Jungmann never claimed that the liturgy is anything other than an act of worship, it is easy to read into his work a view of liturgy as primarily a pedagogical initiative. In the proposal to learn from and draw on a particular period of Church history, Jungmann was also risking the charge of antiquarianism. While there is a certain degree of truth in his assessment of the "vivid catechesis" of early Christianity, it is hard to deny the charge of a selective reading of history with little recognition, for example, of the vibrant educational and catechetical developments of late antiquity and the early Middle Ages.

These limitations should not blind the modern reader to Jungmann's contribution to catechesis as a worthy field of study. Recent thinking has developed his original focus on liturgy as the

---

14 See also Willey, de Cointet, and Morgan, *The Catechism of the Catholic Church and the Craft of Catechesis.*

framework for the Rite of Christian Initiation for Adults (RCIA). Furthermore, the important place of liturgy in the wider catechetical framework is now recognized in the mainstream of Catholic thought.[15]

By the 1930s, catechetical thought was embarking upon a phase of far-reaching development that would continue throughout the rest of the century. The two-stage reform of method and content reflected the Church's dialogue with other disciplines (method) and its willingness to draw on its own resources in order to address the challenges of the age (content). Catechesis was thus to become a distinct field of study with its own history and an associated need to develop and rediscover its own validatory theoretical corpus. By the middle of the twentieth century there is little sense of religious education understood as other than a process of integral faith formation, rooted in a catechetical vision but part of the timetable and framework of the Catholic school. More importantly, there is still no hint of catechesis and religious education as separate, although related, conceptual fields, as is found in later magisterial documents.

Concluding Remarks to PART I

Catechetical processes have moved in tandem with wider church and sociocultural movements. In the early Church, faith formation was centered on the family and the wider church community, in a context of faith nurture. In time this approach was enhanced by greater awareness of the insights offered by Greek philosophy. The work of Augustine offers a synthesis of the relationship between nurture and scholastic frameworks of catechesis. In the Middle Ages, catechesis retained its roots in the worshipping community and became a component of the *renovatio* of Charlemagne. The rise of the Scholastics ensured that it developed a more cutting educational edge. In the years following the Council of Trent, the Catholic Church organized its catechetical endeavors to strengthen church

---

15 *General Directory for Catechesis*, 50, 71, 85, 87, 257, 258.

identity in the face of the Protestant Reformation. This was the age of the Roman Catechism and the rise of the Jesuits and the De La Salle Brothers. Finally, the catechetical renewal of the early twentieth century reformed both the content and the method of catechesis. It set the scene for the insights offered by the Second Vatican Council and the subsequent teaching on catechesis and education developed in the later years of the twentieth century.

This set of historical contexts has demonstrated that the contemporary understanding of catechesis and religious education as distinct concepts does not find strong support in the history of Catholic thinking on education. The terms *catechetical paradigm* and *educational paradigm* have been used to identify the key moments in this historical journey. The second half of the twentieth century is when the broader articulation of these separate, although related, conceptual fields emerges.

PART II

CATECHESIS AND RELIGIOUS EDUCATION IN THE CONTEMPORARY CHURCH

Up to the early years of the twentieth century there was scant evidence of any firm conceptual dichotomy between catechesis and religious education. This arrangement remained in place until the final quarter of the twentieth century when Catholic thinking began, cautiously at first, to consider a new alignment between these concepts. The major shift in Catholic thinking in the years following the Second Vatican Council (1962–1965) had a profound effect on the conceptual framework of religious education. During this period, religious education developed in response to two currents: the first was the rediscovery of the Christian community (or parish) as the principal site for the diffusion of the Church's catechetical mission; the second was the rise of new thinking about liberal models of religious education that contested the concept of faith nurture as an integral component of the school syllabus in an increasingly pluralist society. By the first decade of the twenty-first century, the historically conditioned interplay between the catechetical and educational paradigms of religious education had evolved into a fresh understanding of how both concepts were at the heart of the Church's educational mission. This development is charted as follows:

- developments in catechesis and liberal religious education (chapter 5);
- the magisterium's response to the new thinking in catechesis (chapter 6);
- renewing religious education (chapter 7); and
- religious education: the response of the magisterium (chapter 8).

CHAPTER 5

DEVELOPMENTS IN CATECHESIS
AND RELIGIOUS EDUCATION

The method and content reforms of catechesis of the late nineteenth and early twentieth centuries were followed by a third wave of catechetical reform influenced by the broader educational currents of the age. The new thinking about liberal religious education rejected confessional approaches in favor of a more academic study of religion and associated ways of thinking.

The Anthropological Model of Catechesis

The anthropological model of catechesis captured the post–World War II sense of expectation and hope arising from the growth of education and schooling in the industrialized world. There remained, however, a profound ideological debate in the West over the merits of so-called progressive educational thought. These new ideas in education fostered more inductive (student-centered) as opposed to deductive (content-centered) approaches to learning. Within these highly charged political and cultural contexts, new catechetical ideas continued to draw inspiration from the Catholic reform movements of the early twentieth century, which had sought to refresh Catholic thinking in the light of the supposed practices of early Christianity.

The anthropological model of catechesis had two key frames of reference. First, it reflected a concern that the kerygmatic school's seeming overemphasis on the proclamation of the Good News might be interpreted as an anti-intellectualist stance favoring a sentimentalism at the expense of knowledge of a body of received doctrine.[1] Second, it aimed to tackle the allegedly unreceptive attitudes of students, a situation not wholly unrelated to the social and cultural conditions in which many lived. This challenge was best addressed, it was argued, by making contact with people in all social conditions and responding to the pastoral challenges arising from levels of material and cultural poverty that impeded any efforts at genuine evangelization.

A series of International Catechetical Study Weeks served as the intellectual and pastoral engine for this new thinking. The Study Weeks were spread across the years 1959–1968 and the chosen locations of Nijmegen (1959), Eichstatt (1960), Bangkok (1962), Katigondo (1964), Manila (1967), and Medellin (1968) provided an international backdrop.[2] The agenda of the Study Weeks began with the initial aim of the adaptation of the kerygmatic movement to the wider objective of the reform of the Church and its structures. What made this time particularly interesting is the juxtaposition between the Study Weeks and the important events of the Second Vatican Council and beyond. It seemed that the sense of optimism and hope of the post–World War II world had influenced Catholic thinkers to freshen church teaching to meet the signs of the times and the needs of postwar society.

An example of this push for change was the opening of the "Third World" of Africa, Asia, and Latin America and the consideration of how to address the pastoral and social challenges facing the Church and wider society on those continents.

Gaudium et Spes provides a primary example of the acceptance in the Church of the thinking behind the anthropological method of

---

1 Jim Gallagher, *Soil for the Seed* (Essex, UK: McCrimmon, 2001).
2 Marthaler, "The Modern Catechetical Movement in Roman Catholicism," 77–91.

catechesis. Its opening paragraph outlining the "joys and the hopes, the griefs and the anxieties of the men of this age, especially those who are poor or in any way afflicted" reflects a desire on the part of the Church to align itself with political and cultural shifts in postwar Europe that sought a common home free from the conflicting ideologies that had produced two wars in the space of half a century.

The Study Weeks were influenced by two interrelated but by no means univocal intellectual currents. First, they reflected some of the more radical educational theory of this time, which drew on the behavioral sciences as a means of channeling educational outcomes toward the development of the skills and attributes deemed necessary for the continued support of the postwar social and economic settlement. Second, they were inspired by the corpus of Catholic social teaching, which sought to include improvements in education as part of a mission to improve the living conditions of the poor.[3]

The Study Weeks also offered an ecclesial forum to educationalists like Paulo Freire (1921–1997) who had vigorously challenged the "banking model" of education for preserving a perceived unjust cultural and economic status quo.[4] Freire's thinking was a more radical interpretation of the broader tradition of Catholic social teaching.[5] Within such a wider context, the Study Weeks highlighted the strong political dimension to catechesis. The Medellin Study Week of 1968, for example, located the Church's catechetical work within the its broader commitment to social justice; the South American context

---

3 Pope Leo XIII, *Rerum Novarum* (1891).

4 Freire used the "banking" image to describe systems of education that, in his view, focused too much on education as the transfer, or deposit, of knowledge from teacher to student—as if the student were a blank canvas. Paolo Freire, *Pedagogy of the Oppressed,* trans. Myra Bergman Ramos (New York: Continuum, 2000).

5 John Elias, "Whatever Happened to a Catholic Philosophy of Education?," *Religious Education* 94, no. 1 (1999): 92–110. The desire to address economic and social inequalities anticipates some of the impulses behind Pope Benedict XVI's *Letter for the World Day of Peace* (2012).

facilitated an interface between catechesis and the emerging theologies of liberation circulating in South America at that time.

Furthermore, the early Study Weeks floated the concept of *preevangelization* as a way of preparing people to hear the Gospel.[6] Fr. Alfonso Nebreda (1926–2004), a Jesuit priest and the director of the East Asian Pastoral Institute, clarified further the principle of preevangelization in the context of the new models of catechesis: "The guiding principle of pre-evangelization is anthropocentric because we must start with the individual as he or she is."[7] This short and important sentence by Nebreda encapsulated the direction in which the catechetical debate was heading. It shows some overlap with the Freirian focus on the liberation of the human person from perceived unjust structures.

The anthropological model recognized and gave credence to the various social, cultural, and political realities faced by the Church around the world. It drew on the Freirian model of education to propose catechesis as an active agent of ecclesial and social change. In the early 1960s, the Second Vatican Council acted as an official ecclesial forum for the discussion of such views. Many of the ideas emanating from the anthropological model were expressed in its published teachings. In the years following the council, the growth of the experiential model offered the Church another perspective on catechesis.

The Experiential Model of Catechesis

The experiential model sought to reorientate catechesis away from the understanding of divine revelation as principally the communication of a set of theological propositions toward one

---

6 Luis Erdozain, "The Evolution of Catechetics: A Survey of Six International Study Weeks on Catechetics," in *Source Book for Modern Catechetics*, ed. Michael Warren (Winona, MN: St. Mary's Press, 1983), 86–109.

7 Alfonso Nebreda, "East Asian Study Week on Mission Catechetics," in Warren, *Source Book for Modern Catechetics*, 52.

predicated on recognition of the life experience and history of the student. In this new model, and in keeping with the student-centered focus of the anthropological approach, the student was no longer understood as a tabula rasa on whose spirit the words of the Gospel and the Roman Catechism would be written. Critics of this form of catechesis claimed (with some justification, it would later emerge) that assorted sociological factors (for example, personal history and identity) were perceived as being of greater importance than the receiving of an inherited faith tradition.[8]

The experiential model was a reaction to the alleged dominance of the concept of salvation history that Jungmann had made the core of his catechetical work. This model had remained at the heart of the Second Vatican Council's document on divine revelation, *Dei Verbum*, published in 1965. The experiential construction of catechesis built on the anthropological model and drew on the Second Vatican Council's call for dialogue with other religions to develop a theory of catechesis with wider implications. Put briefly, if the Church were to accept that some elements of the truth were located beyond its boundaries, did it follow that Truth could not be identified solely with the Church's body of received teachings?[9]

The experiential method also recalled the pedagogical reforms of the early twentieth century (for example, the Munich Method), which had, in turn, drawn on the emerging insights of developmental psychology to improve the dialogue between catechist and student. Furthermore, the experiential model sought to redress the perceived

8 Joseph Ratzinger, "Handing on the Faith and the Sources of the Faith," in Joseph Ratzinger, Godfried Danneels, Franciszek Macharski, and Dermot Ryan, *Handing on the Faith in an Age of Disbelief* (San Francisco: Ignatius Press, 2006), 13–40.

9 Gabriel Moran, for example, claimed that revelation lay at the heart of the student's own faith history. He rejected the traditional understanding of revelation as a faith tradition to be passed on in teaching and worship. Moran argued that the traditional understanding of revelation as sacred history was no more than a modern construction of the events narrated in scripture. See Gabriel Moran, *Theology of Revelation* (London: Burns and Oates, 1967).

imbalance between the respective emphases on content and method in previous catechetical reforms and allow the student's catechetical experience and personal history to be further enhanced in the light of the new catechetical ideas. In this respect it is questionable whether the experiential method was any more revolutionary than earlier methods of catechetical reforms in that it was looking to reconfigure the relationship between so-called cognitive and affective learning with a view to implementing more effective catechesis.

The determined focus on the personal experience of the student encouraged a reconsideration of the importance of teaching doctrine in catechetical programs. If catechesis had traditionally been focused on the passing on of a revealed tradition of faith, the more explicit focus on the place of human experience could be interpreted as a new direction within the Catholic tradition.

Taken together, the anthropological and experiential models were wide-ranging attempts to make catechesis more fulfilling and integrated by drawing on a range of insights in the field of education. In practice, both schools of thought recognized the range of human experience of those to be catechized. Many of the key principles of these models informed the teachings of the magisterium both in the Second Vatican Council and in the *General Catechetical Directory*, published in 1971.

In summary, the new models of catechesis were designed to improve catechetical practice by drawing both on church tradition and insights arising from other ways of thinking. This took place as the mode of operation of religious education in schools was increasingly questioned by other philosophies and worldviews. This is where it will be helpful to explore the genealogy of religious education.

Genealogy of Religious Education

"Religious education" as the title of a subject in the school curriculum has its origin in a particular religious and social context. In the United States of America in 1903, the Religious Education Association (henceforth REA) was founded as a home for Protestant

Christians who wished to reform what they saw as overly pietistic models of religious formation.[10] In this influential movement, "religious education" (also the title of the Association's academic journal) was the preferred term for the teaching of Christianity in a way that brought together "liberal theology, the social gospel and progressive education."[11] The emphasis on the educational nature of religious education was intended to offer an alternative to "revivalist" tendencies in the Protestant Christian religious instruction of the time. It is here that the roots of a Christian critique of predominantly faith-nurture approaches to religious education are found.[12]

The intellectual thrust of this movement came from a growing awareness of the child as living organism and not as a figure ready to be pressed into any prearranged form.[13] As such, the REA drew inspiration from the wider progressive movement in American education at that time. Religious education in its earliest incarnation was not, and never claimed to be, a synonym for religious instruction, nor for any explicit Christian nurture approaches to religious formation.[14] On the contrary, from its outset it sought to offer a

---

10 For example, cf. Mary Boys, "The Standpoint of Religious Education," *Religious Education* 76, no. 2 (1981): 128–41; Marylin Kravatz, *Partners in Wisdom and Grace: Catechesis and Religious Education in Dialogue* (Lanham, MD: University Press of America, 2010).

11 Kieran Scott, "Religious Education and Professional Religious Education: A Conflict of Interest?" *Religious Education* 77, no. 6 (1982): 587–603.

12 This fertile ideological movement grew in an America where there was a clear separation between church and state. The separation of powers and the resultant distinction between laws and customs seemed to be a driver of a healthy religious pluralism.

13 Two important early texts here are Albert Coe, "Religious Education as Part of General Education," originally published in *The Religious Education Association: Proceedings of the First Convention* (1903), 40–52 and John Dewey, "Religious Education as Conditioned by Modern Psychology and Pedagogy," originally published in *The Religious Education Association: Proceedings of the First Convention* (1903), 60–66.

14 Horace Bushnell's seminal text, *Christian Nurture*, mapped out the key lines of the faith-nurture approach within the American Protestant tradition. See

new experience located in the encounter between religious ways of thinking and the study of education.[15]

While the REA became more influential in American Protestant circles, the Catholic tradition on the whole remained initially unaffected by the issues surrounding the emergence of this new understanding of religious education.[16] In the early years of the twentieth century, there was no hint that school-based religious instruction was anything other than catechesis and, for good measure, linked to the emerging social teaching of the Church.[17]

Pius X emphasized the teaching of doctrine as a means to personal salvation. His encyclical on catechesis, *Acerbo Nimis*, issued in 1905, offered a template for the systematic teaching of Catholic doctrine. Although written some two years after the founding of the REA in America, Pius X saw clear merit in the didactic approach implied by the English term "religious instruction." His own catechism, published in 1908, reflected this way of thinking in its list of simple questions and answers on the key points of Catholic doctrine.[18]

Horace Bushnell, *Christian Nurture* (London: T. Nelson and Sons, 1861). For commentary on Bushnell, see Boardman Kathan, "Horace Bushnell and the Religious Education Movement," *Religious Education* 108, no. 1 (2013): 41–57 and Scott, "Religious Education and Professional Religious Education."

15   William Rainey Harper, "The Scope and Purpose of the New Organization," originally published in *The Religious Education Association: Proceedings of the First Convention* (1903), 230–40.

16   In the early years of the twentieth century, Frs. Edward Pace and Thomas Shields of the Catholic University of America were outlining new approaches to religious education but did not align their reforms specifically with the work of the REA. See John L. Elias, "Thomas E. Shields: Progressive Catholic Educator," in *Educators in the Catholic Intellectual Tradition*, ed. John L. Elias and Lucinda A. Nolan (Fairfield, CT: Sacred Heart University Press, 2009), 75–102; "Edward Pace: Pioneer Psychologist, Philosopher and Religious Educator," in Elias and Nolan, *Educators in the Catholic Intellectual Tradition*, 49–74.

17   Leo XIII, Encyclical Letter *Rerum Novarum*, 1891.

18   *Catechism of Pope Pius X*, 1908. https://www.ewtn.com/catholicism/library/catechism-of-st-pius-x-1286

The thematic link between the teaching of Christian doctrine and social reform was picked up by Pope Pius XI. His encyclical on Christian education, *Divini Illius Magistri*, published in 1929, provided a comprehensive framework for the understanding of Christian education as an integrated program of formation with supernatural aims.

The final paragraphs of the encyclical, however, go in a different direction than that taken earlier in the century by the REA. For Pius XI, any educational method that dispensed with the work of grace and relied on human nature is unworthy.[19] Pedagogical approaches arising from too close a partnership with other worldviews presented major challenges to the Catholic tradition.

The lack of a shared understanding of the role of religion vis-à-vis education between the Catholic Church and the REA can be summarized as follows: in the Catholic tradition, the role of "religious instruction" so called, is to form students doctrinally so that they can enter into dialogue with the world and propose a Christian way of thinking. Conversely, the REA's approach is to see religious education as a fresh discipline which has arisen from insights in other fields of learning and, by implication, offers a model for a new way of understanding Christianity. The divergence in understanding as described here provides an insight into the tension between two distinct interpretations of the aims of religious education within Christianity.

19   Hence every form of pedagogic naturalism which in any way excludes or weakens supernatural Christian formation in the teaching of youth, is false. Every method of education founded, wholly or in part, on the denial or forgetfulness of original sin and of grace, and relying on the sole powers of human nature, is unsound. Such, generally speaking, are those modern systems bearing various names which appeal to a pretended self-government and unrestrained freedom on the part of the child, and which diminish or even suppress the teacher's authority and action, attributing to the child an exclusive primacy of initiative, and an activity independent of any higher law, natural or divine, in the work of his education. (Pope Pius XI, Encyclical Letter *Divini Illius Magistri* (1929), 60.)

In time, increasing Catholic membership of the REA played a significant part in its development as a multidenominational, as opposed to liberal Protestant, organization.[20] There was, however, no parallel Catholic movement to reconfigure approaches to religious education along the lines suggested by the REA. The "method" reforms of the early catechetical renewal movement valued a more structured and educational approach to catechesis; this reflected, albeit dimly, the educational spirit of the reforms undertaken by the REA.[21] The kerygmatic movement, in its drive to recapture a perceived joy in Christian nurture approaches to religious formation, was a clear move in another direction and a rejection of the philosophy underpinning the REA.

The term "religious education," therefore, is a recent arrival in the Catholic lexicon. Catholic thinking had traditionally emphasized the catechetical and instructional nature of any form of religious formation in the school. It is worth noting that the term "religious instruction" appeared frequently in the English translation of the magisterial documents on catechesis and education from the first half of the twentieth century onward.[22] Only later in the twentieth century does "religious education" become the preferred subject title.[23] Indeed, both terms are often used interchangeably alongside

---

20 John Elias, "Catholics in the REA," *Religious Education* 99, no. 3 (2004): 225–46.

21 For more on the reform of Catholic education in the US in the early years of the twentieth century, see Leonardo Franchi, *Thomas Shields and the Renewal of Catholic Education* (Washington DC: Catholic Education Press, 2023). Part II (37–65) is especially relevant for a deeper understanding of the reforms of method.

22 For further thoughts on issues related to translation of key terms in magisterial document on catechesis and religious education, see Leonardo Franchi, "Authentic Religious Education: A Question of Language?," *Religions* 9, no. 12 (2018), special issue, "Reenvisioning Religious Education," online, https://www.mdpi.com/2077-1444/9/12/403.

23 Cf. *General Catechetical Directory*, 19; *The Religious Dimension of Education in the Catholic School*, 66–70; *Circular Letter to Presidents of Bishops' Conferences on Religious Education in School*.

"education in the faith" and "religious training."[24] What is unarguable is that the use of a broad range of terms to describe the processes of religious formation both within and beyond the school illustrates the complexity of the debate over the most appropriate conceptual framework for religious education.

Religious Education as Study of Religion

In the 1960s, the UK-based educationalist Ninian Smart (1927–2001) questioned the value of explicit faith-nurture approaches to religious education.[25] Also on the table for Smart were the possibilities offered by cross-border initiatives in religion and education. This seemed to chime with the Church's desire at that time to build bridges with other religious traditions.[26] Smart's body of work reflected a shift from religious education as Christian faith formation to religious education as a broader study of religious influences on the human condition.[27]

Smart was convinced that religious education in schools would be improved by the opening of its conceptual borders, at that time almost exclusively Christian, to insights into the human condition offered by other religions and their related ways of understanding the world. Smart, whose principal sphere of influence was the

---

24 This varied usage might, of course, reflect the perspectives of the many authors of these documents over a lengthy period; in addition, the role of the translator of magisterial documents cannot be left to one side.

25 Smart initially retained his allegiance to Christianity. For an overview of Smart's religious beliefs, see https://www.newworldencyclopedia.org/entry/Ninian_Smart.

26 The inspiration for this development was *Nostra Aetate*, the Second Vatican Council's Declaration on the Relation of the Church to Non-Christian Religions (1965).

27 Cf. Gabriel Moran, "Religious Education" in *A Companion to the Philosophy of Education*, ed. Randall Curre (Oxford: Blackwell, 2008), 332–41; Gabriel Moran, "The Intersection of Religion and Education," *Religious Education* 69, no. 5 (1974): 531–41; Gabriel Moran, *Design for Religion* (London: Search Press, 1974); Moran, *Theology of Revelation*.

English-speaking world, was affected by the patterns of migration which had reshaped the cultural composition of Western countries and subsequently driven a concomitant growth in new forms of religious worship.

In his desire to change the face of religious education and, in his mind, to strengthen its position in the academic framework of the school, Smart was initially following the reformist lines mapped out by the REA in early twentieth-century America. In this way of thinking, a theologically liberal and educationally progressive model of religious education was the ideal way forward. Nonetheless, the REA's underpinning philosophy retained a Christian worldview. Smart's analysis of the state of religious education led, controversially, to a diagnosis of "schizophrenia," arising in part from the juxtaposition between the dominance of nurture-based religious education in schools and the teaching of religious studies in (secular) institutions of higher education.[28] In response to this situation, Smart proposed an opening of the language and conceptual framework of religious education and theology to wider perspectives and to "the sympathetic appreciation of positions and faiths other than its own. Christian theology, in brief, must be open, not closed."[29]

Smart's overall contribution to debates on the nature of religious education can be grouped into three strands. First, his recognition of the pluralistic nature of society nudged religious education away from a confessionalist paradigm that was ill at ease in this pluralistic society. Second, Smart was in favor of the neutrality of the state in religious affairs in general; this, too, was an indicator of the desirability of nonconfessional religious education. Finally, Smart was convinced that religious education should evolve into a multifaith and academically serious study of religions.

Given the broader multifaceted revolution in religious education that took place throughout the 1970s, what was Smart's overall

---

28 Ninian Smart, *Secular Education and the Logic of Religion* (London: Faber and Faber, 1968), 90.

29 Smart, 91.

contribution to developments in the field? While there is a shared agreement on Smart's status as an influential and hugely important figure in the modern history of theories of religious education, there is still a debate on how positive his contribution actually was.

Two contemporary scholars of religious education, Philip Barnes and Kevin O'Grady, offer contrasting perspectives. Barnes has challenged approaches to religious education that are rooted in Smart's ideas.[30] He agrees that Smart's critique of confessionalism in religious education is both timely and well developed. However it does not follow, claims Barnes, that a phenomenological approach is the best, or even an appropriate, response to the challenges posed by confessionalism. O'Grady, on the other hand, welcomed Smart's ideas on religious education. O'Grady sees the Smartian corpus as a pioneering initiative that made contemporary religious education more academically respectable.[31]

Other and more profound challenges to Smart's legacy have come from a number of angles. To take one example, phenomenology as the parent of cross-religious models of teaching and learning has been deemed inadequate, especially for younger children.[32] An unforeseen legacy of phenomenology, perhaps, has been the removal from the religious education curriculum of the conceptual and linguistic resources needed to combat the global threats to the same liberal values that initially inspired Smart's work.[33]

---

30 Cf. Philip Barnes, "The Contribution of Professor Ninian Smart to Religious Education," *Religion* 31 (2001): 317–19; Philip Barnes, "Ninian Smart and the Phenomenological Approach to Religious Education," *Religion* 30 (2000): 315–32.

31 Kevin O'Grady, "Professor Ninian Smart, Phenomenology and Religious Education," *British Journal of Religious Education* 27, no. 3 (2005): 227–37.

32 John Hull, *Studies in Religion and Education* (London: The Falmer Press, 1984).

33 James Conroy and Robert Davis, "Citizenship, Education and the Claims of Religious Literacy," in *Global Citizenship: Philosophy, Theory and Pedagogy*, ed. Michael Peters, Alan Britton, and Harry Blee (Rotterdam: Sense Publishers, 2007), 187–203.

New Thinking in Religious Education
in the Catholic Tradition

It is a moot point whether the new ideas circulating in the field of liberal religious education influenced the magisterium. A possible explanation for this might lie in the linguistic barriers separating Rome and the key debates in the field of religious education that had taken place principally in English-language academic journals.[34]

While it is unlikely that Smart's thinking had any immediate influence on (or was influenced by) the teachings of the magisterium, his contribution to the intellectual debate on the relationship between religion and education did influence Catholic thinkers like Gabriel Moran (1935–2021). Indeed, Moran's work became a conduit for insights from liberal religious education into Catholic intellectual life, although it would be unwise and unjust to Moran to interpret his substantial body of writings solely in terms of his interpretation of the mind of Ninian Smart. The importance of Moran's work for any discussion on contemporary religious education comes from his Smartian vision of religious education as an academic field with outposts well beyond the confines of the Catholic Church or any other named Christian tradition. Moran's understanding of the nature of religious education needs prefacing, however, by further terminological precision. To be clear, Moran preferred the term "crisis *of* religious education" to "crisis *in* religious education."[35] The former phrase was, he believed, a more meaningful articulation of the need to redefine religious education based on the insights offered by education and rationality. The latter, in contrast, suggested a return to debates on the alleged doctrinal weaknesses of religious education in the post–Second Vatican Council Church.

Moran drew on this terminological distinction to propose a new conceptual model of religious education. He favored "ecumenical education" (the words are included in the title of his book) as the

---

34 This is explored further in Franchi, "Authentic Religious Education."
35 Moran, *Design for Religion*, 12.

descriptor of a new conceptual framework for a subject that would be developed through cooperation between people searching for a truth that is greater than any single truth professed by individual religions. Moran's understanding of "ecumenical" in this case is interesting—he seems to be proposing a model of religious education rooted in a framework transcending any firm attachment to a named religious tradition. For Moran, the benefits of this model included a move away from the *preacher model* (that is, the faith nurture model) of religious education and a willingness to engage with topics other than Scripture and Dogma.

In time Moran took a far more challenging stance against Church-centered religious education. In particular, he labeled traditional religious education "ecclesiastical thought-control for children" and saw the new discipline of religious education as a way to encourage much-needed changes to the structures of organized religion.[36]

Magisterial teaching shows little evidence of Moran's influence. Sr. Finola Cunnane, however, drew on Moran's thought in an attempt to understand better the nature and purpose of religious education for the modern world. Cunnane shares with Moran the view that religious education cannot be a component part of the catechetical process if it is to remain true to its identity as an academic subject.[37] She rejects outright the possibility of accommodation between faith nurture and educational structures. Cunnane's perspective on the academic underpinning of religious education reflects, albeit very dimly, Pope Paul VI's call in *Evangelii Nuntiandi* for "systematic religious instruction."[38] Cunnane proposes an academic process that implies some form of systematic approach, but with a wholly

---

36   Moran, "The Intersection of Religion and Education," 532–33.

37   "Teaching religion in schools is an important aspect of schooling in religious education. Teaching religion in a classroom is an academic process. It is not concerned with initiating people in religious matters. Neither is it preoccupied with teaching a person a religious way of behaving." Finola Cunnane, *New Directions in Religious Education* (Dublin: Veritas, 2004), 136.

38   Pope Paul VI, Apostolic Exhortation *Evangelii Nuntiandi* (1975), 44.

divergent conceptual understanding of religious education and its associated objectives for learning. The focus in contemporary magisterial teaching on religious education is to give pupils "knowledge about Christianity's identity and Christian life."[39] This is a firm response to those that seem to have advocated otherwise.

Cunnane's work summarizes Moran's thinking in a twenty-first-century context. For Smart, Moran, and Cunnane, religious education is best understood as a developing subject that flourishes when liberated from the (perceived) limitations of faith-nurture conceptual frameworks. Alongside this limited model, further radical thinking emerged in the 1970s and '80s. This school of thought sought a suitable template for an educational paradigm of religious education that was distinct from wholly catechetical and faith-nurture frameworks yet recognized the contribution that effective religious education played in the student's faith journey.

39 *Circular Letter to Presidents of Bishops' Conferences on Religious Education in Schools*, 17.

CHAPTER 6

THE MAGISTERIUM'S RESPONSE TO
THE NEW THINKING IN CATECHESIS

The catechetical reform movement was given further impetus by the Second Vatican Council's seeming embrace of the claims made by the Church reform movements of the early years of the twentieth century. The tone of the *General Catechetical Directory*, published in 1971, chimed with the progressive educational thought of the time. In due course, further reforms in catechesis counteracted a perceived deficiency in doctrinal knowledge while retaining some insights from the anthropological and experiential models of catechesis.

The Growth of Inductive Catechesis:
The Second Vatican Council and Catechesis

By the time of the Second Vatican Council, *pace* the insights arising from the catechetical reform movement, the catechetical underpinning of religious education as outlined by Pius XI's *Divini Illius Magistri*, remained the principal conceptual framework.[1] Interestingly, the council did not produce a document dedicated to catechesis. This omission, if we can call it that, seems curious given the intellectual energy surrounding the International Study Weeks

---

1 Pius XI, *Divini Illius Magistri*. To date, this is the only encyclical on education.

taking place around the time of the council. Perhaps the Church was not yet in a position to reevaluate the traditional doctrinal focus of catechesis and was exercising an understandable caution in the face of the new thinking around catechetical matters. Nevertheless, two contrasting points about catechesis emerge from reflection on the wider teachings of the council.

First, the council reminded all bishops that catechesis was their responsibility as chief pastors of the local church. Bishops were called to develop catechetical programs based on the foundations of "holy scripture, tradition, liturgy and on the teaching authority and life of the Church."[2] The focus on the role of the bishop articulates an understandable desire to keep the supervision of catechetical thought within the borders of the faith tradition and, perhaps, limit the influence of other and seemingly more radical voices in the wider debates about the aims and purposes of education.[3]

Second, the wider theme in the Second Vatican Council of openness to other ways of thinking encouraged a reassessment of how best to deal with growing societal change. The claim of openness to the wider world and its associated ways of thinking needs reading from within a broader theological and educational context. In essence, the nature of revelation was at the heart of the discussion. The council's Dogmatic Constitution on Divine Revelation, *Dei Verbum*, had reiterated the traditional understanding of revelation as a set of doctrinal propositions centered on the paschal mystery.[4] This left the Church open to charges of a perceived slant toward an overly cognitive approach to teaching. It is no easy task to reconcile the insights of *Gaudium et Spes* with the more

---

2 Second Vatican Council, *Christus Dominus*, Decree Concerning the Pastoral Office of Bishops in the Church (1965), 14.

3 More recently, Francis has reminded the Church that the life of the believer is "a life lived in the Church"; this ensures that catechesis and theological study are partners in the Church's mission to transmit its heritage to new generations. See Pope Francis, Encyclical Letter *Lumen Fidei* (2013), 22.

4 Second Vatican Council, Dogmatic Constitution on Divine Revelation *Dei Verbum* (1965), 3–8.

traditional view of revelation found in *Dei Verbum*. On the one hand, *Dei Verbum* taught that Truth was found in the revealed doctrine of the Catholic Church, yet in *Gaudium et Spes* there is an openness and a willingness to learn from various situations present in the world. This juxtaposition is further encapsulated in *Lumen Gentium*'s claim there is only one Church of Christ, subsisting in the Catholic Church, while "other elements of sanctification and of truth are found outside its visible confines."[5] Considerable theological acumen is needed to bring such divergent thought into a cohesive whole.

Given these contrasting views and the debates they engendered, it is not surprising that the years following the council saw continued radical thinking on catechesis. There were now steps taken to engage with insights from beyond the Catholic and the broader Christian tradition, as found in the experiential model of catechesis

Responding to the Catechetical Movement:
The General Catechetical Directory

The publication in 1971 of the *General Catechetical Directory* (henceforth GCD) was a landmark occasion. The catechetical reforms that had begun on the fringes of the Church had been gradually—and not without debate—assimilated into church teaching and practice over the twentieth century. This reforming energy had now coalesced into the core of a document which would, in principle, guide all catechetical endeavors for the following twenty-six years. The GCD highlighted the scale of the cultural challenges facing the Catholic Church in the late 1960s and early 1970s and, in response, offered some contrasting lines of thought with Pius X's *Acerbo Nimis*, issued in 1905.

The Second Vatican Council had not mandated a new catechism. It did, however, decree that "general directories" concerning the care

---

5 Second Vatican Council, Dogmatic Constitution on the Church *Lumen Gentium* (1964), 8. It is not possible to do justice to this debate in a short volume on education.

of souls be compiled.[6] The innovative genre of a *directory* was a way of sharing authority with local bishops in fields such as catechesis, in line with the principles of *communio*.

The council was also taking into account broader educational trends that were moving away from an overreliance on codified and centralized curricula toward seemingly more democratic, or decentralized, approaches.

The new genre of directory was not coterminous with catechism. It suggested a text with a looser structure, yet still identified with the authority of the universal Church. The directories would include one with a special responsibility for "catechetical instruction of the Christian people" and deal with all matters pertaining to this enterprise, including the preparation of suitable books.[7] Interestingly, this choice of words does not rule out a new catechism.

The publication of the GCD marked a radical shift away from the traditional use of catechisms in teaching. Following the insights of so-called progressive elements in education, the GCD favored the *inductive* method (emanating from below) over the *deductive* method (emanating from above) of catechesis. It claimed, for example, that the inductive method was an accurate reflection of the original preaching methodology of Christ.[8] While this observation reflected acceptance of the insights of the wider catechetical and educational currents, it did leave the GCD open to accusations of partiality since the teaching methods of Jesus as recorded by scripture cannot be fully identified with any one school of educational thought.

The GCD emphasized the nexus between evangelization and catechesis in the broader context of the pastoral ministry of the Word. It reasserted the role of the wider parish community in catechesis. Although it acknowledged the traditional role of the school in religious formation, it had little to say about the nature of religious education apart from the brief observation that in the older

6 Second Vatican Council, *Christus Dominus*, 44.
7 Second Vatican Council, *Christus Dominus*, 44.
8 *General Catechetical Directory*, 72–74.

Christian countries (meaning Europe), "catechesis often takes the form of religious instruction imparted to children or adolescents in school or outside of school."[9]

This line of thinking can be interpreted in three ways: a) there was no urgent need to reform religious education; b) as a document dedicated to catechesis, the GCD did not see a school subject as falling within its terms of reference; and c) catechesis and religious education (or instruction) were synonymous concepts, with the only difference being one of location. There is an element of truth in each of these observations.

Pius X had recalled the Council of Trent's framework for catechesis in which parish priests had been encouraged to develop wide-ranging catechetical programs to counter the widespread religious ignorance of the time.[10] The GCD, however, moved in a different direction. It saw the need to move beyond an improved in-house catechesis in order to address the wider cultural challenges facing the Church. The shift in emphasis would seem to be a recognition that the catechetical renewal called for by Pius X had failed. The GCD affirmed the position of those who had advocated new models of catechesis as a way of countering the perceived deficit in Christian formation arising from older models.

The GCD also marked the move from Catholic uniformity to inculturation arising from the influence of the anthropological and experiential models of catechesis, as advocated in the 1960s. The renewal of catechesis became a priority for the Church and responsibility for the implementation of the new thinking was given to local Bishops Conferences.[11]

---

9 *General Catechetical Directory*, 19.

10 Pius X, Encyclical Letter *Acerbo Nimis* (1905), 11–12.

11 The new role of Bishops' Conferences had originated in the Second Vatican Council's reorientation of the decision-making processes of the Church. Its support for the formation of a Synod of Bishops was a recognition of a perceived need to appear more open to the emerging Church in the developing world and to be less centralized in its decision-making processes. A good example of the contribution of a Bishops' Conference to the

The growth of this more inductive method of catechesis did not go unopposed. By the middle of the 1970s, the magisterium had begun, cautiously at first, to reassess the shape of catechesis and the importance of teaching doctrine.

The Recovery of Religious Instruction

By the late 1970s, the Magisterium had sought to recover a more deductive model of catechesis in order to counteract perceived deficiencies inherent in the new catechetical methods that had emerged in the years following the council. At the heart of this move was a concern over the seeming downgrading of traditional doctrinal instruction.

The recovery, so to speak, of a more didactic (or deductive) approach to catechesis took place in four related stages:

(i) Paul VI aligned catechesis, evangelization, and religious instruction in his 1975 apostolic exhortation, *Evangelii Nuntiandi*;

(ii) Pope John Paul II cautioned against forms of catechesis that, in both content and method, did not reflect the teaching of the magisterium;

(iii) the genre of the catechism returned with the publication of the *Catechism of the Catholic Church* in 1992 and the *Compendium of the Catechism of the Catholic Church* in 2005; and

---

catechetical debate was the Italian Bishops' Conference's publication of *Il Rinnovamento della catechesi* (Conferenza Episcopale Italiana, 1970): https:// catechistico.chiesacattolica.it/il-rinnovamento-della-catechesi/. This document was translated into English under the title *Teaching the Faith: The New Way* (Catholic Bishops' Conference of England and Wales, 1973). The introduction to this document reflected a desire to maintain an integrated vision of education. There was, as yet, little hint of future developments in the conceptual framework of religious education in the Catholic school and its relationship with catechesis.

(iv) the publication of the *General Directory for Catechesis* (GDC) in 1997 harmonized the various strands of catechetical thought.[12]

Let us explore each of these four stages in more detail.

(i) Catechesis and Evangelization

The important role of the bishops in the development of strategies for evangelization and catechesis was further highlighted by Paul VI's convocation of two important synods of bishops.

The first of these synods met to discuss evangelization and led to Paul VI's *Evangelii Nuntiandi*. In this document, the pope issued a heartfelt call to locate the Church's catechetical mission within the broader picture of evangelization. Interestingly, he defined catechetical instruction as a means of evangelization to serve the whole Church.[13] In this important text, Paul VI reminded the Church that the body of teaching that it had received should be preserved and taught afresh to new generations using the best pedagogy on offer.

The call for "systematic religious instruction" was a warning against forms of catechesis that veered too close to experientialism. For Paul VI, catechesis found its roots in the traditions of the past

---

12 The publication of the *Directory for Catechesis* in 2020 was an attempt to recover some energy around catechesis.

13 A means of evangelization that must not be neglected is that of catechetical instruction. The intelligence, especially that of children and young people, needs to learn through systematic religious instruction the fundamental teachings, the living content of the truth which God has wished to convey to us and which the Church has sought to express in an ever richer fashion during the course of her long history. No one will deny that this instruction must be given to form patterns of Christian living and not to remain only notional. Truly the effort for evangelization will profit greatly—at the level of catechetical instruction given at church, in the schools, where this is possible, and in every case in Christian homes—if those giving catechetical instruction have suitable texts, updated with wisdom and competence, under the authority of the bishops. (Paul VI, *Evangelii Nuntiandi*, 44.)

but remained in need of constant development. Given the suspicion, and at times hostility, in educational circles of the 1960s and '70s to traditional forms of teaching and learning, the advocacy of "systematic religious instruction," with its suggestion of a course of studies taught didactically, was (and remains) a profoundly countercultural statement.

This methodological preference recalled the deductive approach and tone of the Roman Catechism. It recognized the many layers of tradition in the Church's own history while retaining the notion of episcopal authority over the approval of suitable texts. In recalling the Church's commitment to the teaching of its own doctrinal heritage, Paul VI also put down a marker against those who wished education more broadly to be less "traditional" and more "progressive."[14] Without doubt, this was a radical position to take at the time.

More broadly, *Evangelii Nuntiandi* followed the GCD of 1971 in blending what were the traditionally separate but related concepts of evangelization and catechesis into one process of Christian formation. This conceptual revision acknowledged the place of the school in religious formation, while situating catechesis primarily in the wider processes of evangelization. Given that the traditional framework of Christian initiation had positioned catechesis subsequent to evangelization, the reconfigured approach was a reflection of new thinking in the field. Significantly, the role of the school in catechesis is not explored in any depth. There is no indication of the future developments that would lead to a reappraisal of the relationship between catechesis and religious education in the school.

(ii) Catechesis as an Ecclesial Mission

The Second Synod of Bishops in 1977 had catechesis as its theme and led to the publication in 1979 of John Paul II's apostolic exhortation *Catechesi Tradendae*. John Paul II followed Paul VI in recognizing

---

14 See Bowen, *A History of Western Education*, 3:543–50.

the challenges arising from weak forms of catechesis. He regarded effective catechesis as an indispensable feature in the Church's ongoing implementation of the work of the Second Vatican Council.

Regarding catechesis and the Catholic school, John Paul II affirmed that "the school provides catechesis with possibilities that are not to be neglected."[15] This line of thinking is clearly informed by *Evangelii Nuntiandi*'s comments on the nexus between catechesis and the school.[16] It mirrors the GCD's portrayal of catechesis within the school setting and reminds the Church that the Catholic school should offer high-quality religious instruction as part of its curricular offerings.

In order to develop catechetical processes, John Paul II proposed a balanced methodology that eschewed routine and embraced genuine renewal from within the ecclesial tradition. In practical terms, he called explicitly for a rediscovery of "the human faculty of memory" as a way of integrating "the great events of the history of salvation" into the collective consciousness of the Church, thus recalling the early Church's focus on the *narratio* as a pedagogical method.[17] In so doing, he reiterated Paul VI's call in *Evangelii Nuntiandi* for a "systematic religious instruction" to preserve the memory of the Christian tradition at the heart of the Church. John Paul II, however, goes a stage further in advocating memorization as a tool of catechesis alongside dialogue, silence, and written work.[18] Again let us not underestimate how radical a proposal this was at the time.

John Paul II identified both the successes and the limitations of the new thinking in catechesis. He recognized the challenges arising from an eclectic approach driven in part by individual catechists' selection

---

15 John Paul II, *Catechesi Tradendae*, 69.
16 Paul VI, *Evangelii Nuntiandi*, 44.
17 John Paul II, *Catechesi Tradendae*, 55.
18 This blend of methods accords with the broader notion of education as the exploration of the treasures of human knowledge, in contrast to methods that are overly driven by predetermined outcomes.

of what was, and was not, important. Given the wider educational climate of the time, it is no surprise that many in the Church viewed with suspicion moves to regulate such matters in line with a perceived traditionalist approach to teaching.[19] John Paul II, however, argued that a loose approach to catechesis was not in keeping with authentic catechetical tradition; indeed, he hints at the necessity and indeed the desirability of some form of normative text to limit more speculative approaches to catechesis and theological study.[20]

(iii) *The Catechism of the Catholic Church:* A Normative Text for Catechesis

As noted above, the anthropological and experiential models of catechesis had not been universally welcomed in the Church. There was a perception that the post–Vatican II catechetical focus had been weighted too heavily in favor of a *horizontal* (or overly inductive) dimension that, in its more extreme manifestations, regarded the systematic teaching of revealed Christian doctrine as an unwelcome leftover from the so-called pre–Vatican II Church. The then cardinal Joseph Ratzinger shared the views of those who sought a reshaping of the catechetical landscape in order to counter widespread religious illiteracy. In particular, he expressed profound regret at the removal of the genre of the catechism from religious teaching and the related questioning of the relationship between method and content in catechesis.[21]

---

19 This highly contentious topic is covered in Michael Wrenn, *Catechisms and Controversies: Religious Education in the Postconciliar Years* (San Francisco: Ignatius Press, 1991) and Michael Wrenn and Kenneth Whitehead, *Flawed Expectations: The Reception of the Catechism of the Catholic Church* (San Francisco: Ignatius Press, 1997).

20 "Thus, no true catechist can lawfully, on his own initiative, make a selection of what he considers important in the deposit of faith as opposed to what he considers unimportant, so as to teach the one and reject the other." John Paul II, *Catechesi Tradendae*, 30.

21 Ratzinger, "Handing on the Faith and the Sources of the Faith," 16.

In response to the general concerns raised about the level of doctrinal awareness, the Synod of Bishops of 1985 recommended the publication of a new catechism to serve as a point of reference for all future catechisms, or compendia, of doctrine throughout the Church.[22] This recommendation reflected John Paul II's call in *Catechesi Tradendae* for the introduction of some form of normative doctrinal text to serve as point of reference for catechists.

The *Catechism of the Catholic Church* (henceforth CCC) was eventually published in 1992. As the Roman Catechism was written in the context of, and indeed called for by, the Council of Trent in the sixteenth century, the CCC was written in the context of the reforms mandated by the Second Vatican Council and the GCD's call for the preparation of new catechetical texts.[23]

The primary audience of the CCC is the bishops of the Church and, by extension, all priests and those with an interest in catechesis. This is similar to the claim of the Roman Catechism to serve as a manual for parish priests, but the CCC has a wider scope: its target audience is all catechists. In the claim to serve as a reference point for catechisms composed in other countries, there is a recognition of the universal-local dimensions of the Church.

Although the CCC allowed greater freedom to local churches to compose their own catechisms, the CCC's historical significance lies in its (at the time) countercultural exposition of a body of revealed doctrine to be placed at the heart of the catechetical life of the Church.[24] It is hence an official response to Paul VI's call for the

---

22 "Very many have expressed the desire that a catechism or compendium of all Catholic doctrine regarding both faith and morals be composed, that it might be, as it were, a point of reference for the catechisms or compendiums that are prepared in the various regions." Second Extraordinary Synod of Bishops, The Final Report (1985), II (B), A4. https://www.ewtn.com/catholicism/ library/final-report-of-the-1985-extraordinary-synod-2561.

23 *General Catechetical Directory*, introduction.

24 There is no sense that the *Catechism of the Catholic Church* was intended to be a centralized doctrinal straightjacket; on the contrary, it is written as a reference book for catechists and not as a template for all forms of catechesis.

recovery of strong forms of religious instruction. It seemed that the catechetical landscape had shifted toward an embrace of more deductive models.

The magisterium heeded its own advice to use the CCC as a primary source for other catechetical texts. The publication of the *Compendium of the Catechism of the Catholic Church* in 2005 illustrated the ongoing development of catechetical thinking.

There are three points worth noting here. First, as a derivative text, the *Compendium* followed the order and structure of the CCC but reconfigured the doctrinal sections to create a question and answer–style text designed to facilitate memorization of short doctrinal statements. While this reflected John Paul II's call for "memorization," it also raised the legitimate question of whether a more cognitive approach to religious instruction was a denial of the perceived benefits arising from the anthropological and experiential models of catechesis.

Second, the *Compendium* was explicit in its use of religious art as a pedagogical tool. This was a reminder of former times when art illustrated the stories of scripture for the mainly illiterate Church congregations. With the inclusion of this traditional catechetical methodology, the *Compendium* broadened its appeal and complemented the use of the memory and the associated cognitive dimension of catechesis.

Finally, the *Compendium* included a section of prayers. This placed the apparent cognitive dimension of learning in the wider context of Christian prayer, acknowledging that the ultimate purpose of learning is, for the Christian, a right relationship with God arising from a balance between the cognitive and affective dimensions of learning.

Before the publication of the *Compendium*, the Church had already addressed the need to support the doctrinal pillars of the CCC with a revised set of pastoral directives for catechesis. The new directory was a timely and comprehensive map of the challenges and opportunities that the Church needed to address in order to support all involved in the vital task of religious formation.

(iv) *The General Directory for Catechesis:* Exploring Catechetical Methods

If the GCD was a partner volume to the teachings of the Second Vatican Council, the *General Directory for Catechesis* (GDC) of 1997 was a companion volume to the CCC. It was a necessary updating of the earlier GCD in the light of developments in educational and catechetical thought. Following its parent publication of 1971, the GDC recognizes the limits of the genre of a catechetical directory. It can offer no more than broad lines of pastoral guidance.[25] In this vein, it directs its vision to the bishops of the Church and all involved in catechetical initiatives, with the expressed hope that it would serve as a reference point for future catechetical texts, including the publication of local directories and catechisms.[26]

The GDC affirms the delicate balance between catechesis as both a necessary element of evangelization and a transmission of a body of doctrine.[27] While criticisms of a "light touch" doctrinal focus in the 1970s and '80s had some validity, the wider pastoral approaches advocated by the anthropological and experiential approaches to catechesis were not to be too easily discarded.

It is important to note that there is little indication in the GDC that catechesis was synonymous with, or even related to, religious education. The few paragraphs afforded to the role of the Catholic school in catechesis reflect the primacy of the wider Church community (the parish) and not the school, as the center of the catechetical enterprise.

---

25 *General Directory for Catechesis,* 9.

26 *General Directory for Catechesis*, 11.

27 "The publication of the Catechism together with the aforementioned interventions of the Magisterium necessitated a revision of the *General Catechetical Directory* so as to adapt this valuable theologico-pastoral instrument to new situations and needs. It is in service of the entire Church that the Holy See now seeks to collate this heritage and to organize it systematically in order to make it available for catechetical purposes." *General Directory for Catechesis*, 7.

The role of the Catholic school is dealt with in two paragraphs (259–60) in the final section of the document under the heading "Catechesis in the Particular Church." This section affirms the important role of the Catholic school in the life of the Church and draws on *Catechesi Tradendae*, where the vital function of religious instruction in the Catholic school had been emphasized.[28] There is little sense here of a school-based catechesis model, and the recognition given to both catechesis and religious instruction offers a wider ecclesial context for their respective modes of operation.[29]

It needs, of course, to be borne in mind that the GDC was written after the magisterial documents on education had proposed that catechesis and religious education be considered as separate although related enterprises. The explicit recognition of the distinction shows a common approach as between the Congregation for the Clergy (the "author" of the catechetical directory) and the Congregation for Catholic Education (the "author" of the documents on education). The dual approval, so to speak, lends considerable weight to the established magisterial distinction between catechesis and religious education.

The renewed focus on the parish as the key locus of faith formation raised further questions about the role of school in the religious nurture of young people. This led to a rethinking of the conceptual framework of religious education and its relationship with catechesis and the wider Church.

---

28 "Religious instruction in schools is developed in diverse scholastic contexts, while always maintaining its proper character, to acquire different emphases. These depend on legal and organisational circumstances, educational theories, personal outlook of individual teachers and schools as well as the relationship between religious instruction in the schools and family or parish Catechesis." *General Directory for Catechesis*, 74.

29 "Christian education in the family, Catechesis and religious instruction in schools are, each in its own way, closely interrelated with the service of Christian education of children, adolescents, and young people." *General Directory for Catechesis*, 76.

CHAPTER 7

RENEWING RELIGIOUS EDUCATION

In the time between the Second Vatican Council (1962–1965) and the publication of the *General Catechetical Directory* in 1971, the new thinking in catechesis began to effect some modest reform in the development of religious education. This is the seed of a renewed understanding of the contours of the subject.

Catechesis and Religious Education:
An Uneasy Relationship

The nature of the relationship between catechesis and religious education came under critical scrutiny in the years following the publication of the GCD in 1971. This took place against a twofold backdrop: a) the traditional faith-nurture approach to a school subject seemed increasingly out of place in a pluralist society, and b) internal church reform had shifted the catechetical focus away from the school and toward the family and the parish.

Brother Gerard Rummery's *Catechesis and Religious Education in a Pluralist Society*, published in 1975, brought what had been a specialized debate on the fringes of the Catholic world into the mainstream of Catholic intellectual life.[1] Rummery's book was the

---

1 Gerard Rummery, *Catechesis and Religious Education in a Pluralist Society* (Sydney: EJ Dwyer, 1975).

first comprehensive map outlining the nature of the relationship between catechesis and religious education. This volume was soon followed by more focused, albeit derivative, conceptual maps of the field of religious education as understood in various Christian traditions.[2]

The title of Rummery's book suggests a balanced exposé of two broad concepts. There is a laudatory preface by Ninian Smart: this gives a clue to Rummery's overall thematic direction. An *imprimatur* and a *nihil obstat*, however, seem to anchor the book firmly within the Catholic tradition. Both factors combine to give the reader a sense of anticipation about an innovative approach to reconciling insights emerging from liberal models of religious education with the doctrinal and educational traditions of the Catholic Church.

The keystone of Rummery's position was the need to strengthen the educational foundations of religious education. He argued that religious education needed a strong academic rationale in order to flourish in the school curriculum. Rummery was aware of the tensions arising from the juxtaposition between catechetical frameworks of religious education and the reality of the pluralist society in which the Catholic school operated. This clearly echoes the line of thinking adopted by Smart, as we have seen. Rummery's position can be summarized as follows: catechesis is an integral part of a wider range of activities that belong to the category of religious education, but the difference between catechesis and other forms of religious education is one of kind, not degree. For Rummery, educational paradigms of religious education are underpinned by cognitive and intellectual approaches which leave the individual free to choose a religious affiliation from an informed position.

Rummery proposed an educational paradigm of religious education as a "platform towards faith." This was another way of

---

2 Cf. Kieran Scott, "Three Traditions of Religious Education," *Religious Education* 79, no. 3 (1984): 323–39; Mary Boys, "Religious Education: A Map of the Field," in *Education for Citizenship and Discipleship*, ed. Mary Boys, (New York: The Pilgrim Press, 1989), 98–129.

articulating the concept of preevangelization which had emerged from the International Catechetical Study Weeks. Rummery's book hence opened Catholic intellectual life to the possibility of a renewed vision of religious education.

A succession of theorists developed and critiqued the line of thinking proposed by Rummery. Writing from a nonreligious perspective, the British social theorist, Paul Hirst (1946–2003), wrestled with the philosophical and educational implications of how to harmonize competing religious worldviews with a secular society. It is no surprise that he proposed a sharper and more rationalist edge to school-based religious education.[3] Hirst claimed that the ends of education are always a response to truth, either as the product of natural reason or from revelation. In the clash between revelation and reason—with reason understood as the autonomy of human knowledge—the latter will always have the upper hand. When this criterion is applied to models of religious formation, he concluded as follows: catechesis cannot be predicated on natural reason; education cannot proceed on the basis of faith (revelation); hence there is a need to separate reason and faith, education and catechesis. The resultant model of education is, Hirst claimed, consistent with the Church's own tradition favoring the autonomy of the disciplines.[4]

Hirst's critique of confessional approaches to religious education carries some intellectual weight. He rightly identified the limitations of religious education and broader Catholic educational approaches that fail to recognize the role of reason across the disciplines. Hirst's proposals, however, suggest that the deep-rooted suspicion toward catechetical models of religious education has been translated into a mistrust of the Catholic school and, indeed, any religious underpinning to education. Hirst's sharp division between reason and revelation, while helpful as an initial entry-point into the debate over the relationship between the educational and catechetical paradigms

3 Paul Hirst, "Education, Catechesis and the Church School," *British Journal of Religious Education* 3, no. 3 (1981): 85–93.
4 Hirst, 85–93.

of religious education, ultimately serves as an exit from the Catholic tradition of faith and reason as partners in the search for truth.

The philosopher Michael Leahy (1953–) took this debate a stage further. He argued that the use of the school classroom for purposes other than education, understood here as a critical appraisal of curriculum content, was illegitimate and, consequently, a violation of the public space of the classroom.[5] At the heart of this analysis was a philosophical rejection of insights from revelation being transmitted within the classroom setting. Paradoxically, Leahy was open to the possibility of catechetical initiatives rooted in the wider life of the Christian school; indeed, he claimed that such initiatives should be more explicit. What is not clear in Leahy's analysis is how it is possible to reconcile a commitment to a wholly autonomous classroom to an overall school ethos inspired by or promoting some form of religious faith.

Alongside the ongoing philosophical reappraisal of the roots of religious education and the broader division between educational and religious uses of the classroom, there was considerable thought afforded to ways in which the educational dimension of religious education as proposed by Rummery could be reconciled with the broader catechetical mission of the Catholic school.

The Apostolate of the Classroom

Writing during the years of the Second Vatican Council, Monsignor Eugene Kevane (1913–1996) claimed that the traditional catechetical approach to religious education could be contained within a sound academic setting. Kevane rejected any division between the educational work of the school and processes of religious nurture.

In *Augustine the Educator: A Study in the Fundamentals of Christian Formation*, published in 1964, Kevane held up the educational vision of Augustine of Hippo as a model for the contemporary Church.

---

5 Michael Leahy, "Indoctrination, Evangelization, Catechesis and Religious Education," *British Journal of Religious Education* 12, no. 3 (1990): 137–44.

Kevane claimed that in Augustine's vision all education was a formation in holiness; the study of the liberal arts, philosophy, and theology was part of a framework that combined both study and prayer in one model of formation.[6] There are two substantial points from Kevane's comprehensive work that, interestingly, show crucial lines of convergence with Graham Rossiter.

Kevane described the teaching of religion in the Catholic school as the "apostolate of the classroom."[7] The juxtaposition of two terms that later thinkers would separate conceptually highlights the difference in approach between the more radical thinkers on the educational paradigm side of the debate and those who sought to retain a strong catechetical focus in the classroom. Kevane argued that the professional nature of the religious education course demanded the same degree of thoroughness as other subjects. Religious education, for Kevane, is more than a timetabled space for prayer and related pastoral activities—he argued in favor of demanding programs of religious and spiritual formation. Unlike Rossiter, Kevane seemed more comfortable with the language of catechesis, as demonstrated by his use of the terms "apostolate of the classroom" and "living catechesis" as descriptors of religious education.[8]

Kevane's work is wholly consonant with Catholic catechetical and educational principles. In assessing his contribution to the debate, however, it is hard to dislocate his work from the period in which it was written. Kevane was writing at a time when the practical reality for catechesis and Catholic education was very much that of a Catholic school firmly encased within the traditional home/school/parish triangle. Given that Kevane was writing in the mid-1960s, there remains a question of the suitability of this model for contemporary Catholic schools with pupils from many diverse religious backgrounds. This is not to reject his argument qua

---

6 For more on this theme, see Franchi, "St Augustine, Catechesis and Religious Education."

7 Kevane, *Augustine the Educator,* 304.

8 Kevane, 304, 314.

argument but to identify the shifts in cultural capital differentiating the decades of the early twenty-first century from the middle decades of the twentieth century. In short, the changing social and cultural makeup of the Catholic school population cannot be ignored in our efforts to freshen our models of religious education.

Kevane's work is a valuable reminder of how a traditional view of religious education can, from its natural home in the language and conceptual framework of catechesis, cross the border separating the so-called educational and catechetical paradigms.

Catechesis and Religious Education:
A Creative Divorce

A new direction in the debate was spearheaded by Graham Rossiter (1943–), an Australian De La Salle Brother. He introduced the term "creative divorce" to describe what he regarded as a wholly desirable separation between catechesis and religious education.[9] In diagnosing this "lack of fit," he concluded that a conceptual separation ("creative divorce") would allow for a more authentic catechesis and an academically robust religious education program that would make a more meaningful contribution to the catechetical mission of the school.

Rossiter's ideas remind us that the reductio ad absurdum of the catechetical paradigm is the loss of subject status of religious education, leading to its becoming solely a space for catechetical activities without an obvious academic anchor. What makes Rossiter a significant voice in the debate is his desire to construct a model of religious education with clear theological and academic scaffolding. He recognized that sharp divisions between catechesis and the pastoral life of the Catholic school, on the one hand, and religious

---

9 Graham Rossiter, "The Need for a Creative Divorce between Catechesis and Religious Education in Catholic Schools," *Religious Education* 77, no. 1 (1982): 21–40.

education as a curriculum on the other were artificial boundaries separating distinct but related approaches to one body of knowledge.

For Rossiter, religious education should show congruence between an academically credible approach and a desire to foster the emotional and affective development of young people.[10] This intellectually coherent approach made religious education a serious subject in the curriculum and, in consequence, a major contributor to the overall development of the pupil's religious faith.

Other Catholic thinkers, however, took a different slant. This group valued a firm educational apparatus yet saw no reason to separate this model from a commitment to faith formation. Their work offers an interesting perspective on the developing conceptual journey of religious education.

A Permanent Catechetical Education

While Kevane was writing *Augustine the Educator* in the early 1960s, he would have been unaware, obviously, of the intensity of future debates on the nature of religious education. Thomas Groome (1945–), however, recognized the fraught and delicate nature of the landscape of religious education.

In broad terms, Groome saw great value in the use of the language of catechesis in Christian religious formation. For Groome, it is important to rediscover the traditional meaning of the key terms employed in the debate. He defines the work of religious education as a process that looks at the transcendent dimensions of our life on earth.[11] He suggests that any educational endeavor which enables people to engage in learning about the transcendent merits the title "religious education." It is a valuable term, he claims, with *religious* pointing to its specificity in the world of religion and *education* to its

---

10 Graham Rossiter, "Perspectives on Change in Catholic Religious Education Since the Second Vatican Council," *Religious Education* 83, no. 2 (1988): 264–76.

11 Rossiter, "The Need for a Creative Divorce," 22.

commonality with wider educational principles. Christian religious education is religious education localized within the sources and practices of a specific religious community.[12]

There is much to commend in Groome's understanding of the Christian community as an educational agent. Groome seems to stop short, however, of applying his ideas to the Catholic school and the plurality of worldviews present in it. This limits the full application of his often valuable insights to the subject of religious education in contemporary Catholic schools.[13]

Groome accepts the classic definition of catechesis as the activity of reechoing the Christian story that has been transmitted throughout history. It is an instructional activity that was experienced in the early Church as a verbal exhortation and has now fallen within the wider context of Christian formation.

Groome's terminological precision challenged thinking where terms like catechesis and religious education had often been used interchangeably. Groome was laying out the borders of a field on which key debates would take place over the coming decades. By 2001, Groome had expanded his set of definitions to include "catechetical education" as a suitable headline for the most appropriate model of religious education in the Catholic school.[14] This is proposed in the context of the GDC's focus on catechesis as a form of pastoral ministry; for Groome, this is a weakness in need of some major conceptual reworking.[15] The basis for the reworking

---

12 Rossiter, 25.

13 This analysis of Groome's work is necessarily curtailed, focusing on his earlier writings. There is scope for a fresh comparative study of how his work has developed over the years.

14 Thomas Groome, "Conversion, Nurture, or Both: Towards a Lifelong Catechetical Education; A Cautious Reading of the GDC," *The Living Light* 37, no. 4 (2001): 23–25.

15 The GDC's cursory treatment of the value of "instruction," as evidenced by the use of terms like "mere information" and "mere instruction," suggest a downgrading of the academic rigor that, Groome believed, was intrinsic to effective religious education. Cf. *General Directory for Catechesis*, 29, 68.

is a fresh understanding of evangelization, which should now be seen as a continual process of renewal for the whole Christian community. This new direction of travel developed the traditional understanding of evangelization as coming prior to catechesis and, significantly, reflected Paul VI's commitment in *Evangelii Nuntiandi* to "systematic religious instruction." Groome's principal contribution to the debate is to unify the concepts of catechesis and religious education into one rich process of Christian formation.[16] They are related lenses through which the heritage of Christianity is viewed, nurtured, studied, and communicated. He is offering a remedy for any perceived "irrationality" in catechesis: it is this recovery of the partnership between faith and reason that remains significant for the debate today.

Interestingly, Groome's statement that "pedagogy can be realized within a Christian community" allows him to apply a more inductive model to the teaching of doctrine.[17] This is a claim that good educational principles rooted in reason can be applied to the sharing

16   During the past fifty years or so, Catholics have debated whether to use the term "catechesis" or "religious education." Generally, catechesis came to mean the socialization of people into Christian identity, whereas religious education become more the scholarly and reflective study of a faith tradition. I worry, however, about catechesis that shapes people's ecclesial identity without a thorough education in the whole tradition of Christian faith. On the other hand, Christian religious education that informs people's minds but neglects forming their identity in faith is equally troublesome. In other words, a dichotomy between these two is false and debilitating. I see them—catechesis and religious education—as two essential aspects of the same endeavor. Both values—socialization and education—*must be* and with an appropriate pedagogy *can be* realized within a Christian community. This is why I use the term "catechetical education" throughout—to emphasize the need for both. (Groome, "Conversion, Nurture, or Both," 13.)

17   Groome offers his famous "shared praxis" as a methodological channel lying at the heart of his favored model of Christian religious education. A full critique of this approach is beyond the scope of the present book.

of the Christian message. In his advocacy of educationally sound catechesis, Groome is following the lines of argument set out by Paul VI in *Evangelii Nuntiandi* and John Paul II in *Catechesi Tradendae* as well as providing a contemporary application of Kevane's work as discussed above. The logical conclusion to his insights on the relationship between catechesis and religious education is found in the title of his important article *Religious Education and Catechesis: No Divorce for the Children's Sake.*[18] Groome is reinforcing both the catechetical and the educational dimensions of religious education. This is a clear response to Rossiter's earlier proposal of a "creative divorce" in order to promote mutual enrichment and the greater effectiveness of both fields.

To summarize Groome's position, religious education is catechetical in its commitment to developing faith; catechesis is educational because it requires study of doctrine. This accords with previous magisterial statements on the desirability of systematic courses of religious instruction in the Church.

In sum, Kevane, Rossiter, and Groome are three significant voices in the contemporary debates in the field. Together, they have made a significant contribution to the development of religious education in the years following the Second Vatican Council. The following chapter will explore how the magisterium responded to this burst of scholarly energy.

---

18 Thomas Groome, "Religious Education: No Divorce for the Children's Sake," *Catholic Education* 16, no. 4 (2007): 12–14.

CHAPTER 8

RELIGIOUS EDUCATION:
THE RESPONSE OF THE MAGISTERIUM

In 2009, the magisterium responded to the fresh thinking on religious education in its corpus of catechetical and educational documents by making explicit the distinction between catechesis and religious education that had been foreshadowed in the scholarly literature.

Catechesis and Religious Education:
The Catechetical Documents

Church teaching on education was initially unaffected by the issues arising from the debates in academic circles on suitable conceptual frameworks of religious education. It seemed that such debates were encircling rather than penetrating the magisterium. In the 1979 apostolic exhortation *Catechesi Tradendae*, John Paul, as hinted above, saw catechesis as a specific moment in the broader process of evangelization.[1]

---

1 "All in all, it can be taken here that catechesis is an education of children, young people and adults in the faith, which includes especially the teaching of Christian doctrine imparted, generally speaking, in an organic and systematic way, with a view to initiating the hearers into the fullness of Christian life. " John Paul II, *Catechesi Tradendae*, 18.

Although John Paul II had written in *Catechesi Tradendae* about the role of catechesis in the school, he had not mentioned the specific relationship between it and religious education. Some recognition of a minor shift in thinking was evident in 1981 when he commented on the distinct but complementary nature of religious education in the school and catechesis in the parishes.[2] This intervention brought the Church into the heart of a wider academic debate that it had hitherto largely ignored as it continued to draw on catechetical theory as the dominant conceptual framework for religious education.

The unexpected shift in emphasis suggests that the intellectual energy arising from the debates in the wider academic world had effected some modest change in how the Church understood the role of religious education vis-à-vis catechesis. This configuration, however, seemed to keep religious education at arms length from catechesis. John Paul II also claimed that religious education was very much linked to catechesis.[3] This implies that religious education would draw on catechetical ideas either as a source of topics for study or to offer a more extensive curricular support structure.[4]

The publication of the GDC in 1997 brought together catechetical thinking in one comprehensive document. The GDC reinforced both the primacy of the parish community in catechesis

---

2 "L'insegnamento religioso, impartito nelle scuole, e la catechesi propriamente detta, svolta nell'ambito della parrocchia, pur distinti tra loro, non devono essere considerati come separati." Author's translation: "The teaching of religion in schools and actual catechesis carried out within the parish, although distinct, should not be considered separate entities." John Paul II, "Address to the Priests of the Diocese of Rome" (1981), 3.

3 "I wish to encourage you in your efforts to review religious education materials in order to see that they are based on principles of sound catechesis." John Paul II, "Address to the Bishops of Great Britain on Their Ad Limina Visit" (1992), 6.

4 This suggests that, in the pope's mind at least, religious education was little more than an application of catechetical processes in a school setting. Such interventions are evidence of the magisterium's developing understanding of the broader issues surrounding the question of religious nurture in the Catholic school.

and the complementarity between catechesis and religious education (religious instruction), stressing in particular the latter's role in cultural dialogue. For this dialogue to be fruitful, the GDC advised that the intellectual demands of religious education be consonant with requirements in other subjects and thus facilitate an encounter with the "cultural patrimony" promoted by the school.[5] This position is in line with Kevane, Rossiter, and Groome's espousal of the importance of fostering high academic standards in religious education.

The evolving relationship between evangelization and catechesis did not leave the debate on religious education unaffected.[6] Religious education's unique contribution to evangelization seemed to lie in the teaching of a distinct body of knowledge within the school setting. While the GDC had little to say about the place of catechesis in schools, its key contribution to the debate is an affirmation of the separate conceptual frameworks of religious education and catechesis.[7]

This call to complementarity built on the Congregation for Catholic Education's initial definition of these terms' distinctive identities in 1988 (see below) for the purpose of ensuring that

---

5 *General Directory for Catechesis*, n. 22.

6 The realignment was further enhanced by Benedict XVI's Motu Proprio *Fides per Doctrinam*, issued in 2013, which transferred competence for catechesis from the Congregation for the Clergy to the Pontifical Council for Promoting New Evangelization: "Faith needs to be strengthened through teaching, so that it can enlighten the minds and hearts of believers. The particular moment of history in which we are living, marked as it is by a dramatic crisis of faith, calls for an ability to meet the great expectations present in the hearts of believers for a response to the new questions being directed both at the world and at the Church." Benedict XVI, Apostolic Letter Issued Motu Proprio *Fides per Doctrinam* (2013). This significant change could be interpreted as a call for catechesis to provide the energy for the future growth of Christianity in the "old" Christian countries.

7 "The relationship between religious instruction in schools and catechesis is one of distinction and complementarity: 'there is an absolute necessity to distinguish clearly between religious instruction and catechesis.'" *General Directory for Catechesis*, 73.

there was little doubt as to their separate fields of operation. It is worth highlighting that the GDC itself questioned models of religious education that drew heavily on catechetical principles.[8] In the magisterial documents on education, however, there is some evidence of a gradually increased awareness of the role that religious education plays in the wider catechetical journey of the student.

Catechesis and Religious Education: The Educational Documents

While the theory and practice of catechesis had been the subject of dedicated magisterial documents, religious education had been considered primarily in the broader context of dedicated educational documents.

The Second Vatican Council had made significant shifts toward an apparent openness to the needs and anxieties of the age. To what extent did this influence thinking on education?

The short conciliar document on education, *Gravissimum Educationis*, while aligning itself with the broader reform agenda of the council, drew heavily on Pius XI's encyclical of 1929.[9] *Gravissimum Educationis* offered a broad focus on the principles of education and hence recognized and accepted the changing social and cultural reality of the postwar world. This cautious engagement with educational reform is encapsulated in the call for a "special post-conciliar commission" with the specific remit to develop the notion of "Christian" education.[10] Nonetheless, *Gravissimum Educationis* would act as a charter for the evolution of Catholic thinking on education despite its reliance on a document by Pius XI which seemed to be at odds with the Second Vatican Council's

---

8 *General Directory for Catechesis,* 73.
9 Indeed, *Gravissimum Educationis* refers to Pius XI's encyclical in twelve of its thirty-six footnotes.
10 Second Vatican Council, *Gravissimum Educationis*, Declaration on Christian Education (1965), 65.

hope for an accommodation with the modern world. Given this broader context, it is no surprise that *Gravissimum Educationis* did not refer at all to the nature of the relationship between catechesis and education: the debate had yet to begin.

Although the GCD of 1971 had opted into the broad conciliar reforms in catechesis, it was some time before the Congregation for Catholic Education's documents began to engage with the need to consider reform in schools. The publication of *The Catholic School* in 1977 signaled the beginning of a faint change of direction in the tone of the debate in its advocacy of "catechetical instruction" in Catholic schools.[11]

The articulation of the place of the family and the wider community in religious formation was a recalling of the catechetical arrangement of early Christianity. The emphasis on catechetical instruction in the Catholic school could be interpreted as either an affirmation of a traditional "catechesis in the classroom model" of religious education or, perhaps, a recognition of the need for catechetical instruction—possibly for the sacraments of initiation—outside the standard school timetable.

Whatever the intention, the tone of the document is urgent, possibly owing to a perception that the catechetical renewal and broader educational reforms were having a detrimental effect on the transmission of doctrine. Following this document, *Lay Catholics in Schools: Witnesses to Faith*, published in 1982, turned the Church's attention to the increasingly important role of the lay (Catholic) teacher. Given the decline in the numbers of religious from apostolic congregations and orders with a dedicated charism for education, the Church had to ensure that lay teachers were well formed doctrinally and pastorally. The integration of the pastoral and the academic

---

11 "It is recognised that the proper place for catechesis is the family helped by other Christian communities, especially the local parish. But the importance and need for catechetical instruction in Catholic schools cannot be sufficiently emphasised. Here young people are helped to grow towards maturity in faith." *The Catholic School*, 51.

dimensions of education provided a helpful context for further development of the relationship between catechesis and religious education in the professional activity of the (lay) Catholic teacher.[12]

The first major exploration of the relationship between catechesis and religious education in a magisterial document came with the publication in 1988 of *The Religious Dimension of Education in a Catholic School*.[13] What makes this text highly influential is its clear articulation for the first time in a magisterial document of the *distinctive* yet *complementary* spheres of influence of catechesis and religious education.[14] This new position reflects both Rossiter's

---

12 *Lay Catholics in Schools* was the application to education and the profession of teaching of the principles of the lay apostolate that had been laid out by the Second Vatican Council in *Apostolicam Actuositatem*. This second part of the educational trilogy focused on the promotion of a distinctive Catholic identity rooted in the synthesis of faith, culture, and life. See 29–31.

13 The broad theme of this substantial document is that all education has a religious dimension, and within this theme there is a major exposition of the aims and principles of Catholic education, an analysis of which is beyond the scope of the present book.

14 There is a close connection, and at the same time a clear distinction, between religious instruction and catechesis, or the handing on of the Gospel message. The close connection makes it possible for a school to remain a school and still integrate culture with the message of Christianity. The distinction comes from the fact that, unlike religious instruction, catechesis presupposes that the hearer is receiving the Christian message as a salvific reality. Moreover, catechesis takes place within a community living out its faith at a level of space and time not available to a school: a whole lifetime. The aim of catechesis, or handing on the Gospel message, is maturity: spiritual, liturgical, sacramental and apostolic; this happens most especially in a local Church community. The aim of the school, however, is knowledge. While it uses the same elements of the Gospel message, it tries to convey a sense of the nature of Christianity, and of how Christians are trying to live their lives. It is evident, of course, that religious instruction cannot help but strengthen the faith of a believing student, just as catechesis cannot help but increase one's knowledge of the Christian message. The distinction between religious instruction and catechesis does not

notion of separate but adjacent fields of operation for catechesis and religious education as well as John Paul II's view of religious education as a space for reflection on the content of catechesis. It rejects sharp conceptual separations while holding onto a degree of separateness in order to avoid a merging of the disciplines of catechesis and religious education.

Paragraphs 67–68 reveal that the perceived dichotomy between catechesis and religious education, which had been the subject of much scholarly writing in the early 1980's, had been finally recognized by the magisterium as an authentic expression of the "Catholic mind" on education. This configuration encouraged the development of a strong academic rationale for religious education in its advocacy of a strong scholastic framework with an approved syllabus, interdisciplinary links. and, when possible, public examinations.

This is further evidence of the strengthening of the educational model of religious education in light of the insights gathered from the wider field of educational studies into objectives, syllabus, and methodology. The religious education curriculum is not, however, a derivative or second-rate catechesis but a body of knowledge with a unique way of analyzing culture and the human condition. The school is hence accorded a unique status as a place of intense dialogue between Christianity and "the world," a position wholly in keeping with the teaching of the Second Vatican Council.[15] Given the

---

change the fact that a school can and must play its specific role in the work of catechesis. Since its educational goals are rooted in Christian principles, the school as a whole is inserted into the evangelical function of the Church. It assists in and promotes faith education. (*The Religious Dimension of Education in the Catholic School*, 67–68.)

15 A second concern is the place of other world religions in the religious education class. Although this dimension of religious education is underpinned by knowledge and not explicit faith formation, it is taken for granted in the magisterial documents that the Catholic school will have the teaching of Christianity as its fundamental point of reference. There is little recognition of the place of other world religions and other ways of thinking in

advances in scholarship and magisterial teaching, it was necessary to produce further guidance on the nature of religious education.

Catechesis and Religious Education: The Circular Letter of 2009

The lack of clear direction in the magisterial teaching of the Church on the concrete nature and curricular shape of the subject of religious education is problematic when set against the thorough magisterial treatment of catechesis, as evidenced by the publication of three directories on the subject of catechesis since the Second Vatican Council.[16]

The 2009 *Circular Letter to the Presidents of Bishops' Conferences on Religious Education in Schools* (henceforth *Circular Letter*) was a groundbreaking, if inadequately reported, initiative. Although the *Circular Letter* is a short document, its status as the first pronouncement by the Congregation for Catholic Education on religious education makes it a key resource for developments in the field.

The *Circular Letter* articulates the key ideas that had been developed across a range of other documents on both catechesis and education.[17] As an initial charter for religious education, it allows the Church's teaching to be more accessible, increases the status of the subject, and, hopefully, works against its misrepresentation as an explicitly catechetical endeavor in a school setting.

The *Circular Letter* presents the relationship between catechesis and religious education in very plain terms. Those unaware of the antecedents of this document would be in danger of interpreting it as a denial of the Catholic school's role in the faith formation of

---

this approach. This leaves the Church open to accusations, whether just or unjust, of a religious exclusivism at variance with the modern and wholly desirable vision of the school as a place of encounter with the "other."

16 This includes the *Directory of Catechesis* of 2020.

17 Cf. *The Religious Dimension of Education in the Catholic School* and the *General Directory for Catechesis*.

the pupils.[18] Dealing with the specific question of the broader school curriculum, the *Circular Letter* calls religious education an essential element in the life of the school: it plays a role in the evangelizing mission of the Church and complements the broader catechetical initiatives in the family and the parish.[19]

In sum, it seems that the arguments advanced by Rossiter for a "creative divorce" had been accepted by the magisterium, yet the closeness of the new relationship shows that Groome's advocacy of "no divorce" had also been influential. This would suggest that the Church is looking for inspiration from more than one intellectual position and is still seeking ways of developing and concretizing this complex relationship. While this openness to scholarship and intellectual life is welcome, is it the case that those responsible for the design of programs of religious education, for now, lack a clear conceptual template?

Looking Ahead

The magisterium responded to changes in the landscape of religious education and allowed its own traditional catechetical approach to religious education to be influenced by new thinking. Of course, the Congregation for Catholic Education could have resisted this call to reform and retained a strict catechetical paradigm within the school as a theological safety barrier against the advance of secularist

---

18 Note the implied distinction between catechesis and religious education in schools in Benedict's address to the bishops of Australia: "All the members of the Church need to be formed in their faith, from a sound catechesis for children, and religious education imparted in your Catholic schools, to much-needed catechetical programmes for adults." Benedict XVI, "Address to the Bishops of Australia on Their Ad Limina Visit" (2011).

19 "Catechesis aims at fostering personal adherence to Christ and the development of Christian life in its different aspects whereas religious education in schools gives the pupils knowledge about Christianity's identity and Christian life." *Circular Letter to Presidents of Bishops' Conferences on Religious Education in Schools*, 17.

ideas. The fact that this did not happen is a significant indicator of openness to new ideas.

The gradual embrace of the educational paradigm reflected the (perennial) call to enter into dialogue with other ways of thinking. It recalled the early years of the catechetical reform movement, with its embrace of insights into processes of learning, culminating in the systematic planning that lay at the heart of the Munich method.[20] Hence, the magisterium was, once again, looking around at developments in the wider world of ideas and assessing whether, and to what extent, they could enhance its own ways of thinking.

The emphasis on a harmonious relationship between catechesis and religious education gives the lie to any claim that a commitment to an educational paradigm precludes any aspiration to faith commitment or faith nurture in the Catholic school curriculum.[21]

On the other hand, a separation between religious education and the broader faith formation of the pupil might be at variance with the Catholic school's broader mission to participate in evangelization. If evangelization is central to the total experience of the school community, there must be limited space for activities which are not part of the mission to evangelize.

Owing to the impact of these issues on pastoral and theological dimensions of Catholic life, they need addressing in a context wider than is provided by the fields of catechesis, education, and religious education alone. Only a deeper and theologically driven investigation of the relationship between catechesis and religious education will allow a satisfactory response to the issues mentioned above. In part 3 we consider how the theological model of the Church as communion (*communio*) can strengthen the relationship between catechesis and religious education.

---

20   See chapter 5 for an outline of the various methods of catechesis.

21   This is similar to the sentiments expressed by Benedict XVI in his "Address to the Catholic Religion Teachers" (2009), where he makes the Christian case for the unity of religious and human formation.

PART III

CATECHESIS AND
RELIGIOUS EDUCATION:
A SPIRITUALITY OF COMMUNION

The notion of unity-in-diversity, a key feature of the theology of *communio*, offers a viable hermeneutic for a renewed and richer understanding of the relationship between catechesis and religious education. To understand the breadth and depth of this term, we here examine the notion of *communio* in the context of tradition and progress. Only then is it possible to glimpse the richness of this term as an interpretive key and make sense of John Paul II's use of the term "spirituality of communion" as the underpinning principle of all formational activities.[1] In keeping with the notion of *unity-in-diversity*, John Paul II describes "spirituality of communion" as a way of making room for and recognizing what is positive in others and welcoming the other as a gift from God. This suggests strongly that *communio* is more than just another ecclesiological model but is, in reality, a dynamic force that underpins and shapes the wider life of the Christian. This argument is set out as follows:

---

1 John Paul II, Apostolic Letter *Novo Millennio Ineunte* (2001), 43.

- What does *communio* mean as a theological expression (chapter 9)?
- What is understood by the term "spirituality of communion" (chapter 10)?
- How can "shared mission" bring together catechesis and religious education (chapter 11)?

CHAPTER 9

EXPLORING *COMMUNIO*

In the opening address to the delegates assembled for the Second Vatican Council, Pope John XXIII spoke of both *tradition* and *progress* as key constituents of the Church's role in the modern world.[1] What did he mean by this choice of words? Essentially, John XXIII was outlining a vision of the council as the latest stage in the Church's "uninterrupted witness." He fully understood the need to develop new ways of teaching and giving witness to the modern world while retaining the "sacred patrimony of truth inherited from the Fathers," yet recognizing the "changing conditions of the modern world." He wanted the Church's body of doctrine (a "sacred patrimony of truth") to be preserved while ensuring that the Church was not regarded as an institution concerned exclusively with preservation of historical traditions for their own sake.

This call for change reflected Saint John Henry Newman's criteria for assessing whether doctrinal developments were authentic or simply the grafting of new ideas onto the Christian worldview. To be sure, all developments in doctrine, if they are to be legitimate, must grow from already-established doctrinal traditions.[2] What is remarkable in John XXIII's opening address is its sense of historical, theological, and pastoral perspective. Alongside the call to conservation of

---

1   Pope John XXIII, Opening Address to the Second Vatican Council, 1962.
2   Newman, *An Essay on the Development of Christian Doctrine.*

Tradition, he emphasized the need to be aware of the demands arising from social and cultural changes in the world. John XXIII thus offered scope for some form of innovation in the Church's mode of engagement with such forces: the call to conserve Tradition was not a summons to retreat behind the walls of fossilized theological ideas.

The Second Vatican Council itself had offered an example of how the tradition/progress relationship could effect substantial reform across many aspects of Catholic life. The Council revolved around the twin axes of *ressourcement* and *aggiornamento* and the fruit of its deliberations was a set of documents that made, and continue to make, a deep impact on contemporary Catholic life.[3]

In the years during and following the Second Vatican Council, ancient terms like "People of God" and *"communio"* were recovered from the worlds of Judaism and early Christianity and reconsidered in the broad context of the relationship between tradition and progress. The theology of *communio* had much to offer Catholic thought at an important juncture in its history. It was the rediscovery of the value for the contemporary Church of an ancient Christian term (*koinonia*– fellowship) and hence reflected the intersection of the twin themes of *ressourcement* and *aggiornamento.*[4]

---

3 A good example of the tradition/progress dialectic is found in the Second Vatican Council's Decree on the Adaptation and Renewal of Religious Life, *Perfectae Caritas*. It captured the dynamic relationship between the need to preserve tradition yet find ways in which the energy of the original charism of an order could provide a fund of restorative energy. "The adaptation and renewal of the religious life includes both the constant return to the sources of all Christian life and to the original spirit of the institutes and their adaptation to the changed conditions of our time." *Perfectae Caritatis*, 2.

4 The reemergence of *communio* as an ecclesiological paradigm (or category) was part of the Catholic intellectual revival of the late nineteenth and early twentieth centuries. The works of the Dominican Yves Congar (1904–1995) and the Jesuit Henri de Lubac (1896–1991), were instrumental in the recovery of the early Church's focus on *koinonia*, and offer it, suitably refreshed, as a model of Church suitable for the modern age. See for example, Henri de Lubac, *The Splendor of the Church* (San Francisco: Ignatius Press, 1956/1986) and Yves Congar, *Diversity and Communion* (New London, CT: Twenty-Third

Communio offered a rich and nuanced vision of the Church. It harmonized the necessary mystical and spiritual underpinning of Catholic ecclesiology with the concrete reality of people on a long and often arduous journey of faith.[5] Furthermore, the apparently wide parameters of *communio* were a shield against particularist, or exclusivist, interpretations of existing models of the Church lacking in any semblance of historical and theological subtlety. This was another step away from the political-society model of ecclesiology that had predominated in the late nineteenth century.[6]

The concept of *communio* is bound to the sacramental traditions of the Church: in Catholic teaching, sacramental communion is the source of, and inspiration for, Christian unity and Christian living.[7] The Pauline image of the Church as the Mystical Body of Christ reflects the vitality of the Trinity of Father, Son, and Spirit. *Communio*, properly understood, allows for grace-filled participation in the life of the Church.

The reemergence of *communio* in the mainstream of Catholic life broadened the theological basis of ecclesiology. While the image of the Church as the Mystical Body of Christ was shaped principally by

---

Publications, 1985) for examples of how this Catholic intellectual revival informed thinking in ecclesiology.

5 Reflection on *communio* offers an image of unity-in-diversity/diversity-in-unity that flows from consideration of the nature of the Trinity. Despite the apparent strengths of the model, the question of unity-in-diversity/diversity-in-unity remains ecclesiologically problematic. While "unity-in-diversity" surely reflects the pastoral intentions of the conciliar and postconciliar documents and offers some scope for outreach and inclusion, matters of Catholic teaching have, by definition, fixed outposts. There is clearly a limit to the diversity of belief and expression that can sit comfortably within any unified body of doctrine.

6 For essential reading on models of ecclesiology, see Avery Dulles, *Models of the Church* (New York: Doubleday, 2002).

7 Chapter 9 of the *Didache* and the *First Apology of St. Justin the Martyr* are possible eyewitness (or participant) accounts of early Christian worship. The latter's account has been included in the text of the *Catechism of the Catholic Church*, para. 1345.

images drawn from Christology, *communio* retained the language of
sacramentality, while offering a theological underpinning from the
doctrine of the Trinity.[8]

Communio allowed the aspect of relationship and dynamism that
is intrinsic to the theology of Trinity, to influence ecclesiological
thought.[9] It opened Catholic teaching to new ways of understanding
the respective role of the priest and layperson and, crucially,
encouraged Catholicism to enter into deeper dialogue with Christian
communities not *in communion* with the Holy See.[10] Here are discerned

8   "The divine persons are relative to one another. Because it does not divide the
     divine unity, the real distinction of the persons from one another resides solely
     in the relationships which relate them to one another." *Catechism of the Catholic
     Church*, para. 235.

9   Avery Dulles sketches out the ecclesiological ideas of John Paul II in Appendix
     1 of *Models of the Church* (2002). This essay is a helpful introduction to the
     place of *communio* in the life of the Church.

10   Even in the beginnings of this one and only Church of God there
       arose certain rifts, which the Apostle strongly condemned. But in
       subsequent centuries much more serious dissensions made their
       appearance and quite large communities came to be separated
       from full communion with the Catholic Church—for which, often
       enough, men of both sides were to blame. The children who are
       born into these Communities and who grow up believing in Christ,
       cannot be accused of the sin involved in the separation, and the
       Catholic Church embraces upon [sic] them as brothers, with respect
       and affection. For men who believe in Christ and have been truly
       baptized are in communion with the Catholic Church even though
       this communion is imperfect. The differences that exist in varying
       degrees between them and the Catholic Church—whether in
       doctrine and sometimes in discipline, or concerning the structure
       of the Church—do indeed create many obstacles, sometimes serious
       ones, to full ecclesiastical communion. The ecumenical movement
       is striving to overcome these obstacles. But even in spite of them it
       remains true that all who have been justified by faith in Baptism are
       members of Christ's body, and have a right to be called Christian,
       and so are correctly accepted as brothers by the children of the
       Catholic Church. Moreover, some and even very many of the signif-
       icant elements and endowments which together go to build up and

the seeds of later ecumenical initiatives that would revolve around applying *communio* to concrete pastoral situations with the Anglican communion and the Orthodox Church.[11]

The Extraordinary Synod of Bishops in 1985 reassessed the nature of the Church in the light of postconciliar developments. In a sense, it acted as "balance sheet for the twenty years of the Council."[12] With regard to the images (or models) of Church that had emerged from the council, the 1985 Synod, crucially, put *communio* at the heart of its thinking.[13] This development marked the early stages of the journey of *communio* to become more than another ecclesiological model: *communio* was now a prism through which other themes could be interpreted.

The value of *communio* as a hermeneutical key was further stressed in 1992 with the publication of *Communionis Notio*, a letter to the bishops of the Church from the Congregation for the Doctrine of the Faith. The purpose of *Communionis Notio* was to restore some

---

give life to the Church itself, can exist outside the visible boundaries of the Catholic Church: the written word of God; the life of grace; faith, hope and charity, with the other interior gifts of the Holy Spirit, and visible elements too. All of these, which come from Christ and lead back to Christ, belong by right to the one Church of Christ. (Second Vatican Council, *Unitas Redintegratio*, Decree on Ecumenism (1964), 3.)

11 See Second Anglican/Roman Catholic International Commission, *(ARCIC II) The Church as Communion* (1991), especially para. 2; the Joint International Commission for the Theological Dialogue between the Roman Catholic Church and the Orthodox Church, *Ecclesiological and Canonical Consequences of the Sacramental Nature of the Church: Ecclesial Communion, Conciliarity and Authority* (2007).

12 Joseph Ratzinger, *Pilgrim Fellowship of Faith: The Church as Communion* (San Francisco: Ignatius Press, 2005), 129.

13 "The Church is sacrament, that is, sign and instrument of communion with God and also of communion and reconciliation of men with one another. The message of the Church, as described in the Second Vatican Council, is Trinitarian and Christocentric." *The Church, in the Word of God, Celebrates the Mysteries of Christ for the Salvation of the World*, The Final Report of the 1985 Extraordinary Synod (1985), 2.

balance to debates on the nature of the Church, a sign perhaps that the proposals of the 1985 Extraordinary Synod had not made a significant impact on Catholic thinking on ecclesiology.

In this letter, the focus on *communio* in the 1985 Extraordinary Synod is revisited owing to a perceived lack of integration into Church life of ecclesiological models such as People of God and Body of Christ. This was a matter of general doctrinal and pastoral importance.[14] *Communionis Notio* is rooted in and reflects on earlier

14 *Communionis Notio*'s key point is the precedence of the universal Church over the local, or particular church.

> The universal Church is therefore the *Body of the Churches*. Hence it is possible to apply the concept of communion *in analogous fashion* to the union existing among particular Churches, and to see the universal Church as a *Communion of Churches*. Sometimes, however, the idea of a "communion of particular Churches" is presented in such a way as to weaken the concept of the unity of the Church at the visible and institutional level. Thus it is asserted that every particular Church is a subject complete in itself, and that the universal Church is the result of a *reciprocal recognition* on the part of the particular Churches. This ecclesiological unilateralism, which impoverishes not only the concept of the universal Church but also that of the particular Church, betrays an insufficient understanding of the concept of communion. As history shows, when a particular Church has sought to become self-sufficient, and has weakened its real communion with the universal Church and with its living and visible centre, its internal unity suffers too, and it finds itself in danger of losing its own freedom in the face of the various forces of slavery and exploitation. In order to grasp the true meaning of the analogical application of the term *communion* to the particular Churches taken as a whole, one must bear in mind above all that the particular Churches, insofar as they are *"part of the one Church of Christ,"* have a special relationship of *"mutual interiority"* with the whole, that is, with the universal Church, because in every particular Church *"the one, holy, catholic and apostolic Church of Christ is truly present and active."* For this reason, the *"universal Church cannot be conceived as the sum of the particular Churches, or as a federation of particular Churches."* It is not the result of the communion of the Churches, but, in its essential mystery, it is a reality *ontologically and temporally* prior to every

teachings of the magisterium; in particular, the teachings of the Second Vatican Council.[15] As such, it serves as a clear indication of how the Church understands *communio* as a hermeneutic of unity that offers avenues for future theological investigation.

Communio challenges any sense of compartmentalization of doctrine: Trinity, Christology, sacramental theology and ecclesiology, for example, are bound together as expressions of the dynamism of the Church's patrimony. It hence provides the theological architecture which allows catechesis and religious education to enjoy a common language of faith while respecting their differing modes of operation.

In this context, the shared language of faith allows the Catholic school to become a place of evangelization where the educational experience is informed by Catholic culture.[16] The relationship between *communio* and the Catholic school finds expression in a vision of the Catholic school animated by its distinct ecclesial nature.[17] In this vision of education, the Catholic school is a Trinitarian and Christocentric community of faith where all are encouraged to live according to the Gospel. The alignment between the mission of the Church and the life, work, and educational goals of the Catholic school comes from the mutual and historically conditioned reciprocity between Church and school.

This model of Catholic education is dependent on the continued existence of committed and well-formed teachers, who are instrumental in shaping the vision and the mission of the Catholic school. The important notion of spiritual capital—the array of faith, traditions, and values that have emerged from the Catholic tradition—acquired

---

    individual particular Church. (Congregation for the Doctrine of the Faith, *Communionis Notio,* (1992), 8–9.)

15 The section headings of the document are helpful as signposts to the principal themes in contemporary ecclesiology: The Church, a Mystery of Communion; Universal Church and Particular Churches; Communion of the Churches, Eucharist and Episcopate; Unity and Diversity in Ecclesial Communion; Ecclesial Communion and Ecumenism.

16 *The Catholic School on the Threshold of the Third Millennium,* 11–14.

17 *The Religious Dimension of Education in a Catholic School, passim.*

by key staff in Catholic schools encourages teachers to be both good professionals and authentic witnesses.[18] Such spiritual capital at the heart of the institution ensures that the Catholic school is shaped by a distinctive faith-based vision of education.[19]

What does all this mean for the Catholic school in a pluralist society? The nature of the dialogue between the Church and public authorities on the provision of Catholic school education is crucial. This dialogue can occur on two levels. First, it can be a politically inspired process that defends the right of Catholic schools to exist within a pluralist educational system. Second, the dialogue can focus on how the Church's rich educational heritage can make a positive contribution to public debates on the nature and purpose of schooling. In the latter model, the Catholic school acts out the politically sensitive role of offering a distinctive vision of education that simultaneously offers philosophical challenges to the foundations of the pluralist society itself.

This model of the Catholic school promotes an integral vision of academic learning and human formation that eschews a narrow focus on academic success or on any other performative indicator. Pope Benedict XVI's reflections on the so-called "educational emergency" articulate a way of thinking that is concerned with broader educational issues, in this case challenges to the exercise of legitimate authority and norms of behavior in society, and not solely respecting matters concerning the operation of the Catholic system.[20]

---

18   Gerald Grace, *Catholic Schools: Mission, Markets, Morality* (London: Routledge Farmer, 2002).

19   See Stephen McKinney, ed., *Faith Schools in the Twenty-First Century* (Edinburgh: Dunedin Academic Press, 2008) for a succinct overview of key issues re "faith schools" in a pluralistic society.

20   Benedict XVI's address to the assembly of the Diocese of Rome in 2007 expressed a profound concern arising from developments in modern educational thought that were, he believed, inimical to the development of truly human values. See Benedict XVI, "Address to the Participants in the Convention of the Diocese of Rome" (2007).

This model of the Catholic school is an innovative way of engaging the Catholic school with contemporary life and gives a radical edge to its relationship with both the state and the surrounding culture. The theology of *communio* places the Catholic school at the intersection of the Church's worldview and the necessary responsibility of the state to oversee educational systems. Within this context, the Catholic school's philosophy is one that seeks to harmonize aspects of *communio* with the mission to educate.[21] In other words, the Church's intellectual heritage overflows into the Catholic school's relations with wider society. The resultant synthesis of faith and culture challenges the settled pluralism of contemporary education as it promotes an educational program coherent with the Catholic worldview. This assists the development of a wisdom that, to a greater or lesser extent, opens pupils' horizons and gladdens hearts.[22]

---

21   On the other hand, because of its identity and its ecclesial roots, this community must aspire to becoming a Christian community, that is, a community of faith, able to create increasingly more profound relations of communion which are themselves educational. It is precisely the presence and life of an educational community, in which all the members participate in a fraternal communion, nourished by a living relationship with Christ and with the Church, that makes the Catholic school the environment for an authentically ecclesial experience. (*Educating Together in Catholic Schools*, 14.)

22 For more on this, see Caldecott, *Beauty in the Word.*

CHAPTER 10

THE SPIRITUALITY OF COMMUNION:
TOWARD A SHARED MISSION

A spirituality of communion, understood as the guiding principle of all formational processes, locates Catholic education firmly within the Church's broader evangelizing mission, yet leaves space for the legitimate diversity which lies at the heart of *communio*. A partner term, "integral religious formation," provides a robust underpinning for the developing relationship between catechesis and religious education within the theological architecture provided by *communio*.

Spirituality of Communion:
A Hermeneutical Key for Catholic Education

The Catholic school is called to be an educational community that forms the human person in integral unity and supports the formation of bonds of communion. John Paul II's proposal for a spirituality of communion hence offers an interpretive or hermeneutical key for understanding more fully the relationship between catechesis and religious education.[1] The emphasis on the Trinity illustrates

1   Before making practical plans, we need to promote a spirituality of communion, making it the guiding principle of education wherever individuals and Christians are formed, wherever ministers of the altar, consecrated persons, and pastoral workers are trained,

the links between theology and the principles, processes, and loci of education. It reveals how theological knowledge of the mystery of the Trinity can be applied to all expressions of Christian life. The relationship between catechesis and religious education follows on from the Church's gradual absorption of the implications of *communio* for wider Catholic life and identity.

Such intellectual and pastoral currents have had a profound influence on the Church's thinking on catechesis. As previously noted, the GCD of 1971 drew on the Second Vatican Council and the fruits of Catholic theological scholarship to make initial links between the Church as *communio* and the field of catechesis.[2] This

wherever families and communities are being built up. A spirituality of communion indicates above all the heart's contemplation of the mystery of the Trinity dwelling in us, and whose light we must also be able to see shining on the face of the brothers and sisters around us. A spirituality of communion also means an ability to think of our brothers and sisters in faith within the profound unity of the Mystical Body, and therefore as "those who are a part of me." This makes us able to share their joys and sufferings, to sense their desires and attend to their needs, to offer them deep and genuine friendship. A spirituality of communion implies also the ability to see what is positive in others, to welcome it and prize it as a gift from God: not only as a gift for the brother or sister who has received it directly, but also as a "gift for me." A spirituality of communion means, finally, to know how to "make room" for our brothers and sisters, bearing "each other's burdens" (Gal 6:2) and resisting the selfish temptations which constantly beset us and provoke competition, careerism, distrust and jealousy. Let us have no illusions: unless we follow this spiritual path, external structures of communion will serve very little purpose. They would become mechanisms without a soul, "masks" of communion rather than its means of expression and growth. (John Paul II, *Novo Millennio Ineunte*, 43.)

2   The Church is a communion. She herself acquired a fuller awareness of that truth in the Second Vatican Council. The Church is a people assembled by God and united by close spiritual bonds. Her structure needs a diversity of gifts and offices; and yet the distinctions within them, though they can be not only of degree but also of essence, as is the case between the ministerial priesthood and the common

influence, implicit at first, grew in importance in parallel with ongoing reflection on the implications of *communio* for contemporary Catholic life. The magisterial documents now began to consider seriously how *communio* had the theological potential to reshape thinking on Catholic education.

An exploration of the key magisterial teaching in this field reveal the growing importance of the relationship between *communio* and education. This came to maturation with the publication of *Educating Together in Catholic Schools—A Shared Mission between Consecrated Persons and the Lay Faithful*, published in 2007. The importance of this document goes beyond the mere exploration of the relationship between the lay teacher and the teacher from a religious order.[3] *Educating Together* finally made explicit the thematic links between *communio* and education that had been largely implicit in Church teaching since the early 1970s.[4] It applies the key aspects of *communio* to Catholic education and hence was as an important thematic bridge between theological reflection on *communio* and Catholic teaching on education.[5]

A crucial feature of *Educating Together* is its description of Catholic education as founded on a "shared mission."[6] As discussed

---

priesthood of the people, by no means takes away the basic and essential equality of persons. (*General Catechetical Directory*, 66.)

3　Congregation for Catholic Education, *Consecrated Persons and Their Mission in Schools* (2002), 4. This document acts as a bridge between *Lay Catholics in Schools* (1982) and Congregation for Catholic Education, *Educating Together in Catholic Schools* (2007).

4　Cf. *Lay Catholics in Schools*, 18, 28; *The Religious Dimension of Education in a Catholic School*, 44, 81; *The Catholic School on the Threshold of the Third Millennium*, 11–13, 18; *Consecrated Persons and Their Mission in Schools*, 15. *Educating Together in Catholic Schools* offers a summary of the important themes of *communio*: the *essence* of the Church and the Church as *icon* of the love of God.

5　*Educating Together in Catholic Schools*, 8–19.

6　The implementation of a real *educational community*, built on the foundation of shared mission and values, represents a serious task that must be carried out by the Catholic school. In this setting, the presence both of students and of teachers from different cultural and religious

in chapter 3, John Baptiste de La Salle had introduced religious brothers as teachers in seventeenth-century France. The growth of other orders and congregations with an interest in education widened the Catholic teaching force beyond the priesthood.[7] In the magisterial documents, a shared mission emerged in response to a drop in vocations to religious orders / congregations with a charism for teaching. Shared mission is thus used retrospectively to describe a situation that had arisen from the decline in vocations to dedicated teaching orders / congregations.

A case could be made that the use of "shared mission" in this case is no more than a necessary and limited intervention in response to the changing demographics of the teaching force. The altered demography of the teaching force in Catholic schools has allowed the Church to reconceptualize the role of the lay teacher. However, this is not the full story, as it also offered an opportunity for the Church to appreciate in greater depth the growing participation of lay people in teaching. Shared mission is an example of the spirituality of communion as applied to education. The Church's acceptance of the principle of a shared mission between the lay teacher and the teacher from a religious order / congregation leaves open the possibility of other ways of understanding the term.

Religious Education: A Shared Mission

How satisfactory is "shared mission" as a descriptor of the relationship between catechesis and religious education? Before going any further, it is necessary to clarify precisely what is understood by this term.

---

backgrounds requires an increased commitment of discernment and accompaniment. The preparation of a shared mission acts as a stimulus that should force the Catholic school to be a place of ecclesial experience. (*Educating Together in Catholic Schools*, 5.)

7 Cf. Tom O'Donoghue, *Come Follow Me and Forsake Temptation: Catholic Schooling and the Retention of Teachers for Religious Teaching Orders, 1922–1965* (Berne: Peter Lang, 2004); O'Donoghue, *Catholic Teaching Brothers*; Hellinckx, Simon, and Depaepe, *The Forgotten Contribution of the Teaching Sisters*.

Shared mission in this context recognizes the contribution of the different participants in the project of Catholic education: the parish, the school, bishops' conferences, and associated Church agencies. The family, of course, remains the irreplaceable influence. Furthermore, Catholic education in most contemporary settings cannot ignore the role of the state, especially where the state is a lead provider and funder of education.

Additionally, shared mission identifies religious education as having roots in both catechesis and in much broader educational influences (see chapter 3). This is in line with the claim of the magisterium that catechesis and religious education are complementary processes. The magisterium has not suggested how the complementarity could be encouraged, far less achieved. The evolution of religious education from "school-based catechesis" to full academic subject status hence remains a work in progress. Nonetheless, reflection on *communio* teases out the principles of the shared mission and helps to identify some points of consonance and dissonance between both fields.

Areas of Consonance between Catechesis and Religious Education

Religious education shares a body of doctrine with catechesis. In the Catholic school, the subject should be taught systematically.[8] This arrangement is a reflection of its roots in catechesis and of the critical engagement with culture that contemporary understandings of religious education are designed to promote.

The Church's deposit of faith aligns the Catholic school with the broader life and mission of the Church. Religious education, as a complement to catechesis, thereby presupposes some form of supportive family/parish structures.[9]

---

8 Compare Pius X, *Acerbo Nimis* (1905), 4, and *The Catholic School on the Threshold of the Third Millennium*, 851 for statements from both ends of the twentieth century on the importance of teaching doctrine satisfactorily.

9 *General Directory for Catechesis*, 225–31.

The knowledge and understanding that lie at the heart of religious education are the fruit of study and personal reflection on the Church's doctrinal heritage.[10] Furthermore, the Church also claims that "there is no separation between time for learning and time for formation, between acquiring notions and growing in wisdom."[11] For example, while memorization is a key component of developing knowledge and understanding, any texts committed to memory are more than providers of religious data: they serve as the primary material on which the student can apply a wide range of pedagogical tools.[12]

Religious education is, therefore, a legitimate development of catechesis in the context of the Catholic school. The question of what is understood by "legitimate development" is crucial to understanding the shared mission. John Henry Newman argued that Christian doctrine could not remain a static and unchanging body of knowledge as this doctrine grew over the course of history. What makes this a process of development, as opposed to one of corruption, of earlier ideas is, he argued, a clear continuity between the later and earlier stages of development.[13] Although Newman was concerned with demonstrating doctrinal continuity between the early (apostolic) Church and the Catholic Church of the nineteenth century, the principles he enunciated can be applied to the relationship between catechesis and religious education today.

The proposal that religious education is a legitimate development of catechesis accords with the Newmanian notion that all developments in Church teaching must have clear roots in (and

---

10 *General Directory for Catechesis*, 154.

11 *The Catholic School on the Threshold of the Third Millennium*, 14.

12 For a very insightful reflection on the role of memory in catechesis, see John Paul II, *Catechesi Tradendae*, 55.

13 Newman, *An Essay on the Development of Christian Doctrine*, chap. 5. Newman identified seven "notes" which evidenced the development of, as opposed to the corruption of, an idea. These seven notes are as follows: preservation of type; continuity of its principles; power of assimilation; logical sequence; anticipation of its future; conservative action upon its past; and chronic vigor.

be implicit in) what went before. The distinction is crucial given the claim above that catechesis shares a body of knowledge with religious education. It is clear that this argument could be skewed to conceptualize religious education as school-based catechesis whereby the shared mission was, in practice, little more than a full-scale migration of the language and conceptual framework of faith development into syllabi of religious education. Magisterial teaching on (Catholic) school-based religious education, however, has moved away from this overtly catechetical approach toward a more nuanced vision designed to offer pupils a clear knowledge and understanding of Christianity and Christian life.[14]

Areas of Dissonance between Catechesis and Religious Education

"Shared mission" is a way of bringing into harmony related but distinct concepts. Their distinctiveness is as important to the debate as their complementarity. Although catechesis is deemed a component part of broader faith development that includes but is not limited to school activity, it is important to clarify how the Catholic school can contribute toward specifically catechetical activity while avoiding an overly catechetical approach to religious education. To what extent is this possible? Nonetheless, this is an area of vital importance given the complex mix of confessional and cultural pluralism increasingly found in the contemporary Catholic school.[15]

The catechetical mission of the school is expressed in its wider life, especially in the availability of the sacraments, retreats, and other apostolic initiatives. This broad and rich area of activity is clearly consonant with the idea that, owing to a decline in opportunities for parish and family catechesis, the Catholic school might be the only site of genuine religious formation for young Catholics in

---

14 *Circular Letter to Presidents of Bishops' Conferences on Religious Education in Schools*, 17.
15 James Heft, *Catholic High Schools: Facing the New Realities* (Oxford: Oxford University Press, 2011).

contemporary society. Much more research is needed to assess how successful the Catholic school is as a site of religious formation when home/parish initiatives are lacking.

The subject of religious education draws on and is inspired by this deep-rooted faith tradition. Its contribution to the catechetical life of the Catholic school lies precisely in its educational credibility as a subject taught within a scholastic framework and promoting a synthesis of culture and life. The subject would boast of the same academic credentials as other subjects: visibility on school timetables; systematic planning of content according to recognized criteria; suitably qualified teachers; due consideration of appropriate methods of teaching and methods of assessment; the provision of suitable graded textbooks and other curricular resources; reporting of achievement to parents and other agencies; and the motivation of pupils.[16]

The arrangement proposed above is a convincing expression of the relationship between *communio* and the shared mission. Catholic doctrine and a consonant worldview are experienced in the interrelated catechetical and scholastic contexts. As this relationship is crucial to the success of the Catholic school, we now have to consider suitable ways of developing the shared mission.

---

16 While Groome has argued (see above) that some form of academic rationale could be beneficially applied to catechetical programs in parishes, a key difference seems to lie in the student audience and the intention of those who teach. The "catechetical audience" gathers with a shared intention of developing faith. How strong this commitment to faith development is for younger children who, for example, have not elected to attend a First Communion program outside of school hours, is a matter of debate. This caveat notwithstanding, there are still clear lines separating this audience from the generality of the pupils in a Catholic school who attend a religious education lesson.

CHAPTER 11

DEVELOPING THE SHARED MISSION

The relationship between catechesis and religious education can be summarized as follows: the aim of catechesis is faith formation; the aim of religious education is knowledge of Christian doctrine and its relationship with wider culture. The latter is hence an *invitation* to, or a *deepening* of, faith, but it cannot necessarily be configured according to catechetical concepts and language. In sum, faith formation is its proximate, not its primary aim.

The relationship has been explored here in the context of the ecclesiological model of *communio*. The application of this particular theological/ecclesiological lens offers an original and granular perspective on the distinctive and fluid nature of the relationship between catechesis and religious education. It serves as a reminder that the frame of reference of Catholic education, although rooted in the desire to offer a solid education to all, is best understood and appreciated by those keen to engage with the Church's theological vision.

Looking Back

Three claims were made at the start of the book. Here are some initial responses to the issues raised at the start of the journey.

1. The relationship between catechesis and religious education is most
    fully understood in broader historical and theological contexts.
    - Church teaching proposes a clear distinction between
      catechesis and religious education. This complementary and
      mutually-enriching distinction has both emerged from and
      fostered a wide body of relevant secondary literature.
    - The study of these rich and varied historical contexts drew
      out the genealogy of the relationship between catechesis
      and religious education through four pivotal periods in the
      history of the Catholic Church. This genealogy exemplified
      the fluid nature of catechesis and the evolving relationship
      between church thinking and broader events in society.
    - The magisterial documents on catechesis, education and
      religious education, while anchored in a fully Catholic
      theological vision, reflect a range of historical, educational,
      and cultural contexts. This confirms the need for the Church
      to engage in dialogue with a wide body of opinion.
    - Religious education, as a term, is a recent arrival in the
      Catholic lexicon. It draws on catechesis but has a distinct
      educational flavor. While it can make a valid and worthy
      contribution to catechesis, its most appropriate conceptual
      framework is as a recognized curricular subject configured
      according to standard academic requirements.

2. The theology of communio offers a suitable framework within
    which the partnership between catechesis and religious education
    can be understood.
    - The application of the theological lens of *communio* to the
      complex relationship between catechesis and religious
      education offers some clarity to both present and future
      discussions on the most suitable shape of the relationship.
    - *Communio*, an ancient theological term recovered in the early
      years of the twentieth century, underpins the notion of
      the Church as a reflection of the Trinity (a communion of
      persons) and a place of encounter with Jesus Christ.

- *Communio* moves ecclesiology beyond the limitations of a "political-society" model of Church and encourages a deeper reflection on how the horizontal and vertical dimensions of the Church influence each other. At the heart of any reflection on *communio*-inspired studies is the need to appreciate unity-in-diversity and, of course, diversity-in-unity. The Church as an instrument of communion offers suitable opportunities for the application of this communion in different parts of its life.

3. Religious education is a dynamic partnership between the principles of catechesis and the principles of Catholic education.
   - The dialogic thread in *communio* can be usefully applied to the relationship between catechesis and religious education. A spirituality of communion, therefore, allows us to conceptualize catechesis and religious education as component parts of a "shared mission."
   - Both catechesis and religious education contribute to an integral *religious* formation emerging from the broader integral *human* formation which lies at the heart of Catholic education.
   - Catholic educators have the responsibility to develop a school syllabus that is theologically orthodox, pastorally sensitive and educationally strong.
   - In partnership with others, Catholic educators should ensure that religious education classes are not isolated from the wider life of the school. Religious education should be part of a wider catechetical and cultural experience undertaken with parishes and other ecclesial bodies.

A Directory for Religious Education

Despite the continual restatement in the magisterial documents of the distinctive yet complementary relationship between catechesis and religious education, there is still no suitable operational model for the subject. Catechists, for example, can draw on the principles laid out in the *Directory for Catechesis* and, before that the *General Directory for Catechesis* and the *General Catechetical Directory*. Catholic religious educators have no such universal template on which to draw.[1]

The field of religious education lacks, at present, a dedicated document of similar status to the established catechetical directories of 1971, 1997, and 2020. The *Circular Letter* of 2009, as we have seen, aims simply to clarify the locus of religious education in the life of the school. Given the existence of a wide range of academic literature relating to developments in liberal (or secular) religious education and the related fact that, unsurprisingly, much of this literature comes from outside the Catholic community, perhaps it is time to consider whether a universal directory of (Catholic) religious education would be beneficial to the Church's dedicated band of teachers. The breadth and depth of knowledge required in religious education both emerges from and contributes to an educational vision rooted in Catholic anthropology. Such an approach has implications for both content and pedagogy in the Catholic school's curriculum.

It is fair to ask how such a proposed directory would look. What would its purpose be?

First, the proposed directory would certainly draw on catechetical principles but set these within guidelines suitable for the vibrant and pluralist nature of contemporary Catholic schools. It would recognize that an overly catechetical approach could potentially weaken the academic status of school-based religious education while acknowledging that approaches too heavily influenced by theories of nonconfessional religious education could dislocate it from the wider Catholic vision of education. The directory would show how religious education has grown from distinct catechetical roots but now has a different, although related, conceptual framework. It would be more than a differentiated version of the *Directory for Catechesis*: its aim would be to enhance

---

1 See also Francis, Apostolic Letter Issued Motu Proprio *Antiquum Ministerium: Instituting the Ministry of Catechist* (2021).

the academic standing of religious education within the Catholic community and beyond.

Second, the directory would synthesize the various references to school-based religious education in existing magisterial documents and set these in a wider academic and pastoral context. This would recognize the key influences of theology and catechesis while identifying the unique position of the Catholic school as a center of Catholic culture.

Of course, the suggestion that there should be a directory could be interpreted as antithetical to the reality of a spirituality of communion. A document that attempts to harmonize the many manifestations of religious education across the world would be hard to achieve. Even if it were achievable, it could be unwelcome to those who would regard it as another mechanism designed to thwart local initiatives. More seriously, it would place at risk the key role of the local bishop in determining the shape of Catholic education and formation in his diocese.

Any possible tension between the universal Church and the local church in this respect can be eased by close examination of the declared scope of both the *Catechism of the Catholic Church* and the *Directory for Catechesis*. Both documents actively encourage local adaptations of their content while reminding all of the need to adhere to shared foundational principles. Any proposed directory for religious education would be similarly constructed: it would present the key features of Catholic theology and its associated sociocultural teachings in a systematic way and, crucially, outline the indicative content and associated pedagogy of a religious education syllabus. This would allow the Catholic school to remain firmly within the *communio* of the Church while serving as a place of meaningful dialogue/encounter with the teachings of the Catholic Church for those belonging to other theological and philosophical traditions.

There is much more to be done in this field. This study will serve as the conceptual basis for wider international studies of the ideal conceptual framework and underpinning principles of syllabi of religious education. Indeed, the territory of religious education and this unique interplay of theology, catechesis, educational philosophy, and cultural studies, now needs to be reproposed as the core of Catholic education. I hope that this volume can be of assistance in this mission.

POSTSCRIPT

The Catholic school is called to retain and indeed celebrate a distinct ecclesial identity. That goes without saying. It must ensure that its educational vision is attractive and, indeed, open to those belonging to other religious and philosophical traditions. The Catholic school, as a civic as well as an ecclesial institution, is a key partner in dialogue on how best to shape *all* educational systems and practices for the future.

There is a need for further exploration of how a properly articulated distinction between catechesis and religious education can offer substantial theological, educational, and pastoral capital for future debates on the place of religion and religious ways of thinking in public life. It is essential to find out how aware parish catechists and serving teachers are of the magisterially sanctioned distinction between wider catechesis and religious education in schools. Following on from this, we need to inquire how this affects, if at all, the manner in which they perform their duties and how they understand their respective roles as catechists and teachers.

To move this debate forward, I propose four questions for further research:

Question 1: How can the Catholic school, while part of the *communio* of the Church, remain a civic institution where all are invited to explore the meaning of a "good life" in a spirit of dialogue and freedom?

Question 2: What is the significance of the local educational context for the relationship between catechesis and religious education? For example, what role does the state play in the operation of Catholic education and how does this inform the shape of the curriculum?

Question 3: How do syllabi of religious education, as configured by a range of local churches and their educational agencies, reflect the magisterial teaching on education?

Question 4: What is the relationship between programs of religious education in the Catholic school and the various catechetical programs offered—not just in sacramental preparation—to children who, for whatever reason, do not, or cannot, attend a Catholic school?

Addressing these questions at a local level would allow for extended research on the evolving nature of the relationship between catechesis and religious education across a variety of contexts.

There can be little doubt that religious education cannot operate successfully without a suitably coherent vision of education and schooling shaping other parts of the curriculum of the Catholic school. The presentation of inherited religious and cultural traditions must be a key component of the contemporary vision of Catholic education in all its manifestations. This allows the Catholic school not just to remain faithful to its own mission but to stand as an example of good pedagogical practice to other models of schooling.

*   *   *   *   *

THE GLOBAL COMPACT ON EDUCATION: REDISCOVERING CHRISTIAN HUMANISM

A commitment to education, central to Catholicism, is rooted in a desire to promote the integral development of all people.[1] It is much more than a desire to catechize the baptized, important as that task surely is.[2] In this light, a term of interest for the Church's

---

1 An initial definition of "integral" is available on the website of the Dicastery for Integral Human Development, where it quotes the *Compendium of the Social Doctrine of the Church* (2004), 13: "The Church [...] intends to propose a humanism that is up to the standards of God's plan of love in history, an integral and solidary humanism capable of creating a new social, economic and political order, founded on the dignity and freedom of every human person, to be brought about in peace, justice and solidarity." https://www.humandevelopment.va/en/sviluppo-umano-integrale/fede-e-sviluppo-integrale.html

2 In these conditions, it is no cause of wonder that man, who senses his responsibility for the progress of culture, nourishes a high hope but also looks with anxiety upon many contradictory things which he must resolve: What is to be done to prevent the increased exchanges between cultures, which should lead to a true and fruitful dialogue between groups and nations, from disturbing the life of communities, from destroying the wisdom received from ancestors, or from placing in danger the character proper to each people? (Second Vatican Council, Pastoral Constitution on the Church in the Modern World *Gaudium et Spes* (1965), 56.)

educational mission is "Christian humanism," which has recently returned to the Catholic educational lexicon by means of its inclusion in the Global Compact on Education, introduced by Pope Francis in 2019. A retrieval of this powerful concept potentially offers opportunities for the Church's accumulated cultural and pastoral traditions to enlighten wider educational trends. How this is done, of course, is another question. There are many possible directions of travel, including a reappraisal of the curricular domain of religious education, the subject of the present volume. In order to offer an initial exploration of how the Global Compact can inform and develop the Church's commitment to religious education, two questions will frame this chapter:

1. To what extent can Christian humanism drive the Church's educational mission?
2. What binds Christian humanism to religious education?

The Global Compact's language and tone offer an open hand to people from other religious and philosophical traditions to share in the Church's desire for integral human development. Much discussion and planning lie ahead, in particular over the impact of the Global Compact on established ways of working in Catholic schools and what it could mean for organizational and curricular reform.

The Global Compact: A Fresh Vision of Catholic Education

The concept of a Global Compact is not new. It presupposes a desire to promote on a global stage a set of ideas and principles that are held to be universally valid. For example, the United Nations,

---

See also Second Vatican Council, Declaration on the Relation of the Church to Non-Christian Religions *Nostra Aetate* (1965), 2: "The Church, therefore, exhorts her sons, that through dialogue and collaboration with the followers of other religions, carried out with prudence and love and in witness to the Christian faith and life, they recognize, preserve and promote the good things, spiritual and moral, as well as the socio-cultural values found among these men."

through its own Global Compact, proposes ten principles for corporate sustainability, managed by the Foundation for the Global Compact.[3] The possibility of a Global Compact on Learning was floated in 2011 in a paper by Jenny Robinson that argued for a rethinking of priorities if education were to have an impact on developing countries.[4] It is within these rather faint parameters, cursorily outlined above, that we can locate the Global Compact that Francis has proposed.

Like all new initiatives, the Global Compact on Education (henceforth Global Compact) requires patient discussion of its key principles if it is to become part of the common vocabulary of education. For Francis, the Global Compact is necessary because humanity is facing an anthropological, not just a cultural, transformation.[5] With this project, he is drawing from the Church's rich educational and cultural heritage to offer wider society a new vision of education.[6]

The aims of the Global Compact are threefold: 1) to place the human person at the center of education, 2) to find the courage to be creative and responsible on how we use our energy, and 3) to train individuals for service to the community. The three aims are couched

---

3 See here for more details: https://www.unglobalcompact.org/. Further discussion of the ideology behind this body is for another time.

4 Jenny Robinson, *A Global Compact on Learning: Taking Action on Education in Developing Countries* (2011). Available at https://papers.ssrn.com/sol3/papers.cfm?abstract_id=3956223

5 "We are experiencing an era of change: a transformation that is not only cultural but also anthropological, creating a new semantics while indiscriminately discarding traditional paradigms." Francis, "Message for the Launch of the Global Compact on Education," *Global Compact on Education Vademecum* (2019), 4. See also Francis, "Video Message on the Global Compact on Education," *Global Compact on Education Vademecum*, 23 (Annex no. 1) where he elaborates on the various crises affecting the world, stressing in particular the importance of "hospitality, intergenerational solidarity and the value of transcendence."

6 Francis seems to be inspired by the principles of both *ressourcement* and *aggiornamento*, although neither is mentioned in the Global Compact.

in language that leaves space for local interpretation of how to embed them into different cultural situations. The aims are then translated into seven commitments: 1) to place the person at the center of every educational program, 2) to listen to the voices of children and young people, 3) to encourage the participation of girls and young women in education, 4) to establish the family as the first and essential place of education, 5) to educate ourselves on the openness to the most vulnerable and marginalized, 6) to find new ways of understanding the economy, politics, growth, and progress and 7) to safeguard and cultivate our common home.[7] Each commitment is then broken down into three categories: Ideas for Reflection, Values, and Suggestions for Educators.[8] This presentational method is designed to make the theory behind the Global Compact and its commitments come to life through discussion and hence offer some ways in which educators can explore its implications for practice.

Each commitment, as an invitation to renew the texture of the Church's social mission in education, deserves a nuanced critique. The first commitment—to place the person at the center of every educational program—is arguably the fulcrum around which the other commitments revolve and, crucially, offers scope for interaction with syllabi of religious education in schools.

The ideas for reflection on the first commitment focus on the importance for education of solid anthropological foundations and the necessity to "form a new humanism to overcome the cultural and anthropological metamorphosis of today's society."[9] Three values are then offered as a way to encapsulate the importance of respecting the dignity of each person, promoting integral formation, and protecting the rights of all. Finally, the suggestions for educators show how the three values could be implemented in the life of educational institutions.

---

7 Global Compact on Education website, https://www.educationglobalcompact. org/en/commitments/.

8 *Global Compact on Education Vademecum*, 11–16.

9 *Global Compact on Education Vademecum*, 10.

Interestingly, the Global Compact tends not to include explicitly religious terminology, leading to the question of the extent to which it is the product of an authentically Catholic vision of education and, by extension, how can it offer a positive influence on religious education. This is where it is necessary to clarify how a fresh understanding of Christian humanism can shape a response to the call to action found in the Global Compact.

Christian Humanism:
The Key to Developing the Global Compact

The key to unlocking the potential of the Global Compact for religious education lies in its subtle introduction of the term Christian humanism. It appears at the end of the seven commitments of the Global Compact, linking it, along with the Word of God, to the inspiration of the Church's social doctrine:

> Finally, dear brothers and sisters, we want to commit ourselves courageously to developing an educational plan within our respective countries, investing our best energies and introducing creative and transformative processes in cooperation with civil society. In this, our point of reference should be the social doctrine that, inspired by the revealed word of God and Christian humanism, provides a solid basis and a vital resource for discerning the paths to follow in the present emergency.[10]

To develop an initial grasp of the pope's use of the term "Christian humanism" in the Global Compact, it is important to be aware of the complex genealogy of the term itself. This will lead, in turn, to a more refined understanding of its potential for Catholic education today. Christian humanism as a concept captures (in part at least) the essential purpose of the Church's desire for an integral

---

10 Francis, "Video Message on the Global Compact on Education," 25.

education, which is essential to the Global Compact and which goes beyond utility and addresses the human desire for happiness and transcendence.[11] Christian humanism is often associated with historical figures such as Desiderius Erasmus of Rotterdam (c.1466–1536) and the associated notion of the cultured, literate, and refined "gentleman scholar."[12] While Erasmus did write scholarly works on educational themes, his immediate contexts could be interpreted as somewhat remote from contemporary concerns.[13]

Francis's call for a return of Christian humanism did not emerge without precedent. Crucially, it recalls Benedict XVI's address to European university lecturers in 2007 in which he made an appeal for a "new humanism" to reshape the culture of the continent:

> The present crisis, however, has less to do with modernity's insistence on the centrality of man and his concerns, than with the problems raised by a "humanism" that claims to build a *regnum hominis* detached from its necessary ontological foundations. A false dichotomy between theism and authentic humanism, taken to the extreme of positing an irreconcilable conflict between divine law and human freedom, has led to a situation in which humanity, for all its economic and technical advances, feels deeply threatened.[14]

---

11 Indeed "humanism" on its own lends itself to so many intellectual and cultural currents—patristic humanism, scholastic humanism, renaissance humanism, Catholic integral humanism, and atheistic humanism—that it can be hard to pin down what it means for the world of ideas. For more on this, see Jens Zimmerman, introduction to *Re-Envisioning Christian Humanism: Education and the Restoration of Humanity*, ed. Jens Zimmerman (Oxford: Oxford University Press, 2016), 2–4.

12 The historian of education, James Bowen, used both Erasmus and Martin Luther to illustrate the key lines of Christian humanism and its relationship to education. See Bowen, *A History of Western Education*, 2:329–76.

13 Richard Rymarz and Leonardo Franchi, *Catholic Teacher Preparation: Historical and Contemporary Perspectives on Preparing for Mission* (Bingley: Emerald, 2019), 27–30.

14 Benedict XVI, "Address to European Meeting of University Professors" (2007).

In this address, Benedict mentions his debt to John Paul II, especially to his encyclical *Redemptor Hominis*. The roots of Benedict's concern can also be traced to the insights of the French philosopher, Jacques Maritain, who, in the years following World War II, clearly articulated the challenge to a Christian worldview from both communism and capitalism, calling for no less than a "new Christendom" in which the human person, filled with divine grace, works for the transformation of humanity "and so brings about—in the degree to which it is possible here on earth and in given historical circumstances—a veritable sociotemporal realization of the Gospels."[15] Maritain's proposal for a new Christendom, while seemingly far from the language of the Global Compact, does seem to be an important contribution to how the Church's social mission can be realized and thus bears a family resemblance to the Global Compact's key thematic lines.

While Christian humanism has a long ancestry, it cannot be easily packaged as a distinct set of educational principles with immediate and universal applicability. It could, however, be interpreted more broadly as a cluster of "certain attitudes and impulses that quickens human awareness in different historical circumstances."[16] Furthermore, a more theologically flavored understanding of Christian humanism potentially offers space for discussion of terms like "communion," "covenant," and "stewardship," which flow from an understanding of the human person as made in the image of God.[17] Christian humanism, therefore, is a bridge between religion (Christianity) and secular life (humanism). It is the gateway to a greater understanding of Christianity's contribution to the world of ideas and as marker of a how Catholic social teaching informs the Church's educational mission.

---

15 Jacques Maritain, *True Humanism*, trans. M. R. Adamson (London: Geoffrey Bles—The Centenary Press, 1946), 86.

16 Zimmerman, *Re-Envisioning Christian Humanism*, 11.

17 John P. Bequette, *Christian Humanism: Creation, Redemption and Reintegration*, rev. ed. (Lanham, MD: University Press of America, 2007), 167.

Christian Humanism and Religious Education

In the Global Compact, education is a critical expression of the Church's social mission. It is the driver of a culture of encounter, a key theme of Francis's papacy.[18] The Global Compact proposes what seem to be secularly inspired educational outcomes that promote the dignity of the human person but remain rooted, albeit implicitly, in the Catholic theological and educational traditions. It is wholly reasonable to ask whether the focus on apparently secular outcomes could lead to a weakening of the Catholic educational project or if it is instead a wise move to invite all people to see the Catholic school as a visible and practical expression of authentically human education. In this state of apparent creative tension, we glimpse a contemporary example of a dialogic process between the Church as a community of belief and the wider society, especially in the West, where religious belief is in a state of flux.

The Global Compact could be a helpful resource for underpinning religious education with, as noted by the Congregation for Catholic Education in 2009, "a vision of the human person being open to the transcendent."[19] Deeper reflection on the value of the first commitment—to place the person at the center of every educational program—will offer some possible lines of engagement for teachers, policymakers, and curriculum creators. The curricular subject of religious education alone cannot underpin the project of Catholic education but offers the raw material that can influence and shape discussions on the wider curriculum. Some practical suggestions now follow:

1.   Reemphasize the important place of Christian anthropology in the project of Catholic education. This is an antidote to more fluid conceptions of the human person that are in vogue in some educational, cultural, and political circles

---

18   Francis, *For a Culture of Encounter*, Morning Meditation in the Chapel of Santa Marta (September 13, 2016).

19   *Circular Letter for Presidents of Bishops' Conferences on Religious Education in Schools*, 18.

in the West. We are all made in the image and likeness of God, created for sanctity but weakened by our flawed human nature. Education, therefore, is the healing process that encourages the human person to live virtuously.

2. To advance the role of Christian humanism in education, the authentic religious and human formation of educators is urgent. Much deeper thinking on how to prepare educators for service in Catholic schools will open discussion about what makes Catholic schools distinctive and how the Catholic educational tradition can influence wider thinking on education. Central to this crucial discussion are issues like the preferred academic site of Catholic teacher formation and the opportunities available for ongoing, systematic academic and pastoral formation, including but not limited to preparation for leadership.

3. The renewal of Christian humanism demands no less than a fresh understanding of the vocation of the laity. It is too easy to package the "lay apostolate" principally as a way to involve more people in the life of church organizations such as parish groups and diocesan initiatives. While such expressions of faith commitment are not to be sidelined, they fail to capture the rich and baptismally rooted concept of the lay vocation as found in the documents of the Second Vatican Council.[20]

---

[20] The apostolate in the social milieu, that is, the effort to infuse a Christian spirit into the mentality, customs, laws, and structures of the community in which one lives, is so much the duty and responsibility of the laity that it can never be performed properly by others. In this area, the laity can exercise the apostolate of like towards like. It is here that they complement the testimony of life with the testimony of the word. It is here where they work or practice their profession or study or reside or spend their leisure time or have their companionship that they are more capable of helping their brethren. (Second Vatican Council, *Apostolicam Actuositatem*, Decree on the Apostolate of the Laity (1965), 13.)

Concluding Remarks

The language of the Global Compact is in line with recent efforts by the Congregation for Catholic Education (now subsumed into the Dicastery for Culture and Education) to offer the Catholic educational tradition as a contribution toward the common good. The focus in Catholic schools has moved from explicitly catechetical concerns toward more educationally focused outcomes; in other words, creating a good school open to all and with a unique vision of the human person rooted in Christian anthropology. In this way, the catechetical mission of the school is implicit—and no less valuable—in the life and curriculum of the school. The Global Compact seems to be an affirmation of this shift in direction.

The use of Christian humanism in the Global Compact is a window into the Catholic intellectual tradition. It an invitation to explore how this distinct body of knowledge can inspire wider educational reform today. Ideally, it will facilitate a desire to embed the Catholic intellectual tradition into the Church's discourse about education and thus offer an increasingly robust intellectual and pastoral foundation for its mission to educate.

APPENDIX II

CATHOLIC EDUCATION: ITS NATURE, ITS DISTINCTIVENESS, ITS CHALLENGES

Gerhard Cardinal Müller

I am grateful for the invitation to speak at the launch of the St. Andrew's Foundation as a new instrument in Scotland for the provision and support of Catholic education and of Catholic teachers, and I wish, first of all, to acknowledge and celebrate the fruitful collaboration and partnership between the University of Glasgow and the Catholic Church in Scotland.[1]

As a visitor from, and a representative of, the Holy See in Rome, it is heartwarming to be standing within the walls of an ancient

---

1 Gerhard Cardinal Müller, then-Prefect of the Congregation for the Doctrine of the Faith, gave this lecture at the launch of the St. Andrew's Foundation for Catholic Teacher Education, University of Glasgow, Scotland on June 15, 2013. This is an abridged version. The full text is available at http://www.gla.ac.uk/schools/education/standrewsfoundation/cardinalmullerslaunchaddress/

university, whose degree-awarding power still stands upon the papal bull of Pope Nicholas V, granted to establish the university in 1451.[2]

It is opportune at this present moment, amidst the rapidly changing state of society, of higher education generally and also of the Church, to reflect on the nature and distinctiveness of Catholic education and on the challenges it both faces and also presents. The substance of my talk today will be to offer some thoughts and reflections on these important areas.

The Nature of Catholic Education

It is not insignificant to note that the vision and practice of Catholic education has, throughout the Church's history, arisen out of a coming together of the Church with various cultures. The very mission of the Church, from its beginnings in the Upper Room in Jerusalem at Pentecost, has been to engage with the culture of the time and to seek to penetrate it with the message of the Gospel. At the same time, the Church has drawn on that culture and its wisdom in order to help articulate her own self-understanding and to facilitate her own life and practice. From the beginning therefore, faith and culture have interacted, even when in certain periods of history, the interaction was more hostile and combative than collaborative.

It is not unknown to any of us that for many decades there have been voices raised against the idea of Catholic education, against the fact of distinct faith schools and increasingly, in today's society, there are great challenges to the very idea of a religious education. Various charges are made, including the suggestion that religious education is a form of indoctrination and is contrary to the prevailing culture of freedom. Faith-schooling is said to mitigate against social cohesion, encouraging intolerance, social prejudice, sectarianism, and even bigotry. Within the Church herself, especially in the light of the call to the Church of recent popes to the mission of new evangelization,

---

2 Papal Bull of Pope Nicholas V, January 7, 1451; https://www.british-history. ac.uk/glasgow-charters/1175-1649/no2/pp31–35.

there are voices questioning the need for a separate Catholic education. Should the Church not encourage a simple engagement with the wider society rather than maintain a separate system of education? Such are some of the questions that remain today as part of the melting pot of debates around educational issues. They will, no doubt, continue to be questions discussed and researched within this very Foundation in the coming years.

What It Means to Be Catholic

I would like to distinguish from the outset two important but different meanings of the word "Catholic" within the debate about Catholic education. In the first place, we may consider "Catholic" to refer to a religious denomination within society and the world at large that is organized as a body of believers who are admitted through baptism and whose membership can be described at the level of family, parish, diocese, national church, and international Church, with her leadership in the Holy See in Rome. From this point of view, Catholic education is acknowledged by both church and state as a fundamental right and primary responsibility of Catholic parents, who are the first educators of their children. In accordance with this fundamental right, the state has the duty and responsibility to facilitate the wishes of Catholic parents to educate their children according to their desire to pass on their faith to their children. Particular national states have sought to fulfill their responsibility in a variety of ways, enshrining within their systems of law different arrangements for this provision but always recognizing the fundamental principle that those primarily responsible for the education of children are their parents.

The Catholic Church also recognizes the rights and duties of parents in the matter of education, and from the earliest times has sought to provide support to parents, not least in the area of religious education. Within the rite of baptism, in which parents seek the gift of faith for their children, parents also express their desire and their commitment "to raise their children in the practice of the Faith." The Church, for its part, has always recognized, as an essential element of its mission, the duty to provide the means for this. As John Henry Newman once wrote: for the Church "to baptise and not educate would be a grievous sin!"

The first justification therefore for the church/state collaboration in the matter of Catholic education is rooted in the universal and fundamental rights of parents.

This leads me to a second meaning of the word "Catholic" that also has important implications for the Foundation whose launch we celebrate today. To illustrate my meaning, I would like to refer back to the great fifth-century saint and classical exponent of Christian education Augustine of Hippo, who wrote a work called *The City of God*. The occasion of the composition was the accusation being made against Christians that they were responsible for the fall of Rome. It was claimed that the beliefs, and more importantly, the practices, of Catholics were inimical to the Roman state and Roman society.

Augustine's response was to argue that far from undermining the state, Catholics practiced religious, moral, and social virtues that precisely upheld the state. The reasons for the civil breakdown were to be found elsewhere; ultimately, within the very heart of man. *The City of God* is a comprehensive volume that in many ways laid the foundations for dialogue between the civic state, the secular world, and the Catholic Church—in Augustine's language, between the "city of man" and the "city of God." He argued that what was best in Roman society had its roots in Plato and Aristotle and great Roman minds who had articulated the truth of the supreme Good as the *telos* or "end" of humanity—this is the Good that leads to happiness. They spoke of the good of the body, the good of the soul (of the mind and the will), and the good of the commonweal (of society).

At the heart of all of these goods was the development of the rational mind in conformity with the truth and the nourishing of the will through the attainment and practice of the virtues, of which justice was seen as primary. The foundation was the human person, in whom they discovered a natural drive toward the discovery of the good and the true. We can recognize in Augustine's analysis the basis of much of the way that we speak even today about educational goals, especially in our concern for the whole person. Nevertheless, there was a problem. In the end, thought Augustine, this philosophy was not enough. Individuals and also society could never achieve the good to which they aspired. It is a perennial problem. The classical philosophy was groping toward an answer.

Augustine argued that Christians belong not only to the City of Man but also to the City of God. Embracing all that was true and good in the classical philosophy, belonging to the City of God brought in a number of new elements that both transformed and completed what was lacking in the classical philosophy and Roman society. In the first place, what is and can be known by the human mind is supplemented and completed by the truth of divine revelation. Like many of the great Christian minds in the early centuries, Augustine discovered in the Sacred Scriptures of the Old and New Testament the element that the classical philosophy, from which he himself came, was groping toward. God revealed himself in the history of the seemingly insignificant people of Israel and then most fully in the person of Jesus Christ.

Knowledge, which in classical philosophy was somewhat confined as a result of limitations within the reasoning human person, is both confirmed and completed. All reality and all truth, including the human person, have their source in the One God. In the history of Israel and in the person of Christ, God reveals his nature and also the ultimate nature and destiny of the human person, created by God in his own image and destined for eternal happiness, the ultimate good of humankind. The person of Jesus Christ is not only the fullness of God's self-revelation and the perfection of man; he is also the place of salvation, the place where the wounds in human nature are revealed and healed.

The Ten Commandments present as moral absolutes those goods that classical philosophy had perceived as the goods of the person and of society. But the Decalogue, and by implication, Greek and Roman philosophy, was in the end a pedagogy leading to Christ,[3] who not only reveals the full meaning of the commandments, but both accomplishes them in himself and provides the means of grace by which the very virtues of Christ become embodied in every other person. In Christ, said Augustine, the life of seeking the truth and living the virtues is realized, even though it means a slow progression in constant need of Christ's forgiveness and healing. Finally, for Augustine, the governing power in the City of God is a threefold love—love of God, love of self, and love of others. Love originates in the mystery of the Trinitarian relationships and is the motivation for Creation, Revelation, and the Redemption in Christ. Within the City of God, love gathers, unifies, and perfects all the human virtues.

If I can summarize Augustine's view of the key characteristics of the City of God, they are firstly faith, by which we have access to God and to the truth that he reveals in Christ; secondly hope, by which, in Christ, human weakness and sin is overcome and earthly goodness and blessedness is made possible and the mystery of eternal happiness becomes a true goal; and finally, love, which provides both the motivation for living and the goal of life without end. It is precisely these three—faith, hope, and love—that are the gift of God, through Christ and the Holy Spirit in the sacrament of baptism. In the City of God, it is these three virtues that, in addition to the natural goods and virtues of the human person, are the heart of education.

We can see, therefore, that the word "Catholic" has a fuller, more inclusive, sense. It implies an overarching philosophy of life, which includes all that is good in the philosophies of societies and human culture. Augustine contrasts citizenship in the City of Man with citizenship in the City of God. This is not a contrast between a worldly and an otherworldly approach, but concerns the breadth of one's philosophy of life and of education.

---

3 Cf. Gal. 3:24–25.

What It Means to Educate

It is time now to turn more specifically to the second word in today's subject—education. Few subjects are more contentious in today's society. Long gone are the days in which, in Christian Europe, there was a synthesis between faith and reason and a unity between the disciplines of various subjects in education, in which theology was seen as the Queen of the Sciences. This was the atmosphere in which this University received its papal bull. It owed a great deal to the writings of the philosopher-theologian Thomas Aquinas. Today there are a multitude of views about what education should be and how it should be carried out. There are views that emerge from modernist and postmodern philosophies and ideologies; others emerge from state and political concerns, not least today because of the crisis in the economies of most European countries; and others from capitalist and market-driven theories and models. Finally, there is the overarching secular tone of society today with its emphasis on materialism and consumerism and the growing acceptance of a relativist stance with regard to truth and morality.

In his recent visit to Scotland and England, Benedict XVI spoke of the serious danger of relativism, which will undermine society and religion and in the end will be detrimental to the human person.[4] A proper understanding of education plays a significant part in providing an alternative to this relativist stance. From the time of Socrates, education has been what the underlying Latin word suggests—a drawing out from the human person, through the training of the human mind, will, and emotions, the ability to perceive and act upon the good and the true. The good and the true stand in some way outside the person; they are transcendent. The human person has a natural drive and curiosity to seek and understand them. A danger in the relativism of modern society is the assumption that human freedom essentially entails creating one's own truth and moral good. Notwithstanding the clear perception of the

4 Benedict XVI visited the United Kingdom in 2010.

flaws within our nature, there are logical absurdities in the relativists'
position: first, in asserting as absolutely true that there is no absolute
truth; second, in maintaining that each person's truth is as valuable as
every other's; and third, in asserting that each person's morality is as
good as every other's. The first represents the collapse of reason; the
second and third, if pursued to their logical conclusion, would lead
to the breakdown of society.

This is not to say that tolerance or human freedom are not values
to be highly esteemed. The problem seems to be that such values are
underpinned by a weak philosophy of life and of education, or at
least one that is unarticulated or not critically examined. The result is
the danger of trying to build society and to educate on the basis of
weak foundations.

Here we touch upon one key element of the goals of higher
education. It is surely part of the enterprise of higher education
that it not simply mirror back the values of the society at large, nor
simply that it produce those who will serve the economy through
excellence in business or industry, science or the arts. An important
element is also the ability to take a critical stance and examine the
underlying assumptions, philosophies, and ideologies in society
today and especially those underlying the very disciplines that higher
education pursues. There are those who will maintain that many of
the disciplines are scientific and value-free. It is not difficult to refute
such a claim. The bigger danger arises when the assumptions and
philosophies are unexamined.

The St. Andrew's Foundation can be a place for critical
engagement with the philosophies that underpin the various ideas
about education, not least within the university itself and also in the
wider society, articulating a philosophy of life and understanding
the nature of education found within the Catholic Church herself.
This understanding is especially enshrined in the various documents
concerning education that have emerged from the Holy See over the
last century. I would like to take a moment to pay tribute to those
who have published *An Anthology of Catholic Teaching on Education*

[editor, Leonard Franchi, Scepter, London, 2007], an excellent volume that brings together the significant Church documents, while indicating at the same time those that more particularly pertain to catechesis and those that pertain to Catholic education more broadly. It would be hard to recommend a better resource for study within this new Foundation.

The Vision Articulated by the Church

Both before the Second Vatican Council and since, the Church has consistently proclaimed the dignity of the human person, and the pattern and destiny for the person that is to be found in Christ. Education has a central place in the assertion of that dignity. In the first place, there are the important teachings of popes Pius X and Pius XI. The particular challenge of their times concerned the extent and nature of the state's involvement in education. The Church had to struggle for her rights in the matter of teaching Christian doctrine in schools. Pius XI's encyclical on Catholic education, *Divini Illius Magistri* (1929), reflects the threat of the complete takeover of education by the state in a number of countries in which ideologies that deny or distort the dignity of the person, such as Communism, Fascism, and Nazism were prevailing. In this hostile climate, Pius XI clearly articulated an alternative vision rooted in the basic rights of parents, explaining and defending the good of the human person as involving happiness and justice in this life, as well as the attainment of the person's ultimate and complete happiness in heaven. Happiness both in this life and definitively in heaven was to be understood and pursued through the life of faith—the life communicated through a properly Catholic education.

The period beginning with the Second Vatican Council has seen, with the establishment of the Congregation for Catholic Education in Rome, the reaffirmation of the Church's teaching on the dignity of the human person and our destiny in Christ. The council was expressly a time of returning to the Church's most ancient and secure sources and of opening itself to the wider world. This was particularly focused on the Church's self-understanding and renewal and her salvific dialogue with the world. The Church looked afresh at the scriptures and the Church Fathers in order to reflect on her own changing situation of being a missionary Church within an environment that was no longer Christian. The Church needed to understand anew her own culture, with a history and a tradition to transmit in a holistic way to her own future generations and to the world.

This process is ongoing and is a continued mining of the rich seams of Tradition. This is the underlying purpose of the Year of Faith that we are currently living in the Church.[5] Benedict's explicit invitation was to discover anew the documents of the council and also the council's primary fruit, the *Catechism of the Catholic Church*. The Catechism essentially represents a statement of Catholic culture expressed in the same structure as the New Testament statement of the culture of the early Church: "And they devoted themselves to the apostles' teaching and fellowship, to the breaking of bread and the prayers."[6]

This notion of the Church's culture implies also its transmission through education and leads to an engagement with the variety of cultures within which the Church finds herself today. The whole concept and project had its roots in the early Fathers of the Church who articulated, as I stated earlier in my discussion of Augustine's *City of God*, a vision of Catholic culture within the context of Greek and Roman society. Christian culture, and its transmission through education, was the Christianization of the Greek concept of *paideia*—a word that is difficult to translate but contains the idea of the holistic formation of the human person (body, mind, and spirit), of the person *within* society and *within* civilization or culture. In its

---

5 Benedict XVI declared a "Year of Faith" from October 11, 2012, until November 24, 2013. This was to mark the fiftieth anniversary of the opening of the Second Vatican Council and the twentieth anniversary of the publication of the *Catechism of the Catholic Church*.

6 Acts 2:42.

baptized form, this process is envisaged as being under the pedagogy of God himself and directed toward a final civilization within the mystery of the Trinity.

It was in this same period both before and after the council that the thought and writings of John Henry Newman were being more widely disseminated, especially with regard to his teaching on conscience and on education. Newman himself was deeply influenced by the traditions of the Fathers, and the notion of *paideia* stood behind much of his educational thought. It is not insignificant that the occasion of the recent papal visit of Benedict was also the time that Newman was beatified. At that time, Benedict said of him:

> I would like to pay particular tribute to his vision for education, which has done so much to shape the ethos that is the driving force behind Catholic schools and colleges today. Firmly opposed to any reductive or utilitarian approach, he sought to achieve an educational environment in which intellectual training, moral discipline and religious commitment would come together. The project to found a Catholic University in Ireland provided him with an opportunity to develop his ideas on the subject, and the collection of discourses that he published as *The Idea of a University* holds up an ideal from which all those engaged in academic formation can continue to learn.[7]

The Nature of the Church as Mystery, Communion, and Mission

The reflection initiated at the Second Vatican Council on Catholic culture and its transmission has found articulation, not only in the constitutions of the Second Vatican Council, and in the catechism,

7 Pope Benedict XVI, Homily at the Mass of Beatification of Venerable Cardinal John Henry Newman, September 19, 2010; https://www.vatican.va/content/benedict-xvi/en/homilies/2010/documents/hf_ben-xvi_hom_20100919_beatif-newman.html

but also in the structure of the Church as Mystery, Communion, and Mission. And its particular application to Catholic education was enshrined in the most recent document from the Congregation for Catholic Education entitled *Educating Together in Catholic Schools*, published in the same year (2007) as the *Anthology*.

It is important to understand what the idea of the Church as Mystery, Communion, and Mission involves. Fundamental is communion—which is another way of expressing Catholic culture and its central affirmation of human dignity as bearing the pattern and the destiny of Christ. Communion comes about through initial conversion to the person of Christ and necessarily leads to communion with everything with which Christ is in communion. In other words, it leads to communion with His Body, the Church, with her life and sacraments and teaching and with each and every person who makes up the Church. Communion with Christ also opens up to us all, as both its origin and its goal, entry into the mystery of the life of the Blessed Trinity. And communion within the Body of Christ and communion with the persons of the Trinity give rise to the mission of the Church to draw all of humanity into this life and culture. Indeed, this is ultimately the mission of the Trinity itself—to draw every created person, through the Church, into participation in the Trinitarian life.

It is in this vision of a truly Catholic culture that the most recent document, to which I have referred, *Educating Together in Catholic Schools,* discusses the nature and purpose of education and in particular the joint activity of lay and consecrated persons within the field of education. The document presents a new and challenging statement both of the human person and of the purpose of education. This new statement is set in the language of communion.

Every human person is called to communion because of his nature, which is created in the image and likeness of God.[8] Therefore, within the sphere of biblical anthropology, man is not an isolated individual,

8 Gen. 1:26–27.

but a person, a being who is essentially relational. The communion to which man is called always involves a double dimension, that is to say vertical (communion with God) and horizontal (communion with people). It is fundamental that communion be acknowledged as a gift of God, as the fruit of the divine initiative fulfilled in the Easter mystery.

This description of the human person is inspired by the Church's understanding and vision of what it is to be a human being and as a response to the present cultural context. Young people are growing up in a world marked by moral relativism, individualism, utilitarianism, and a lack of interest in the fundamental truths of human life. The Church is almost alone, it seems, in being prepared to assert the dignity the human person as bearing the image of God—a vision available to reason and once deep at the heart of Western culture, but which is now generally denied. It is when humans are no longer seen to bear the image of God that human freedom is reduced to mere arbitrary whim, and the pursuit of true value is reduced to a consumerism that never satisfies. The Church must give back to young people the true understanding of their own value, which has been taken from them. And this requires the communication of the Catholic faith concerning our true destiny in Christ. This reproclamation and defense of humanity and its true worth lies at the center of the Church's mission—her calling of all people to their true destiny in Christ. We are duty bound to use every possible opportunity to articulate this vision and form future generations in it.

In the midst of so many diverse and at times bewildering versions of educational aims and processes, the Church has a rich and vital vision to proclaim. At its heart is an ideal of the person as called to love and friendship with God and with fellow humans bearing his image. Catholic education is an expression of a Catholic culture that is ever drawing upon the richness of its tradition and the cultures of the ages, ever seeking to renew and restate itself, and always conscious that it does so within the pedagogical mission of God himself in the world. It is a vision that needs to be heard in the world as the Church seeks to serve the world that God loves. As well as seeking to dialogue with today's society, the Church also seeks to live out and incarnate in every place the vision that by God's grace she articulates. May this new Institute play an important role in the study of this vision, its dissemination for the formation of Catholic teachers, and in the support of the schools in which this vision becomes realized.

INDEX

Also available from Catholic Education Press

Thomas Shields and the Renewal of Catholic Education (Education and Integral Human Development). By Leonardo Franchi. Foreword by Mary Pat Donoghue

Renewing Catholic Schools: How to Regain a Catholic Vision in a Secular Age. Institute for Catholic Liberation Education. Edited by R. Jared Staudt. Foreword by Most Reverend Samuel J. Aquila

Words Made Flesh: The Sacramental Mission of Catholic Education (Adeodatus Series on Catholic Education & Culture). By R. Jared Staudt. Foreword by Patrick Reilly

A Brief Quadrivium by Peter Ulrickson

A Sourcebook for English Lyric Poetry. By John Tomarchio

Patience and Salvation in Third Century North Africa: A Christian Latin Reader. By Sarah Klitenic Wear

Available from The Catholic University of America Press

Renewing the Mind: A Reader in the Philosophy of Catholic Education. Edited by Ryan N. S. Topping

What We Hold in Trust: Rediscovering the Purpose of Catholic Higher Education. By Don J. Briel, Kenneth E. Goodpaster and Michael J. Naughton. Foreword by Dennis Holtschneider

The Virtues by John H. Garvey

A Reason Open to God: On Universities, Education, and Culture. By Pope Benedict XVI. Foreword by John H. Garvey. Edited by J. Steven Brown

The Light of Christ: An Introduction to Catholicism. By Thomas Joseph White, OP

The Intellectual Life: Its Spirit, Conditions, Methods. By A. G. Sertillanges, OP. Translated by Mary Ryan. Foreword by James V. Schall